IT SO HAPPEN 3

Callender's
CLASSICS

REALIZATION STUDIOS

©2013
Estate of Timothy Callender

Cover Art by Timothy Callender

ISBN –13:9781489579973

Published by
REALIZATION STUDIOS
P.O. Box 364
Basseterre. St. Kitts
e-mail sunyer98@yahoo.com

Printed in USA by www.createspace.com

Dedicated to

Frank Collymore

who nurtured the talents of
TIMOTHY CALLENDER

*and was first instrumental
in promoting his work*

*All rights reserved. No part of this publication may be reproduced, stored in a
retrieval system, or transmitted in any form or by any means, electronic,
mechanical, photocopy, recording or otherwise, without prior written
permission from Realization Studios with the exception of
short excerpts used with acknowledgement of publisher
and estate of the author.*

Introduction to *Callender's Classics*

TIMOTHY CALLENDER became a household name in 70's and 80's when his stories were regularly read on radio by the late cultural icons of Barbados, Sir Frank Collymore and Alfred Pragnell.

But his name was also a familiar name in schools as his stories were part of many literature texts used in the study of English. Not only did publishers such as *Longman*, *Nelson Caribbean* and *Heinemann* make a place for him in their anthologies, there were also German translations in their storybooks as well.

Throughout the Commonwealth, his stories are well known and one of them, *An Honest Thief*, was chosen as the example for study at the Commonwealth Short Story Writers Conference in England in the 80's. His story, *An Assault on Santa Claus*, was selected for inclusion in *The Oxford Book of Christmas Stories*.

But with his premature death at 43 in 1989, many of his stories were still unpublished and this anthology hopes to partially correct that. This anthology, **It So Happen 3 – Callender's Classics** - brings together the stories written in Standard English. The conversations of the characters are, however, authentic and retain the 'nature language' - the dialect or Barbadian vernacular.

> *"He was in the forefront of our literary advance and his (dialect) literature restored respectability to Barbadian life."* John Wickham – Nation News Literary Editor

"Easily the best exponent of the art of short story writing Barbados has ever had...he uses the vernacular as one should apply seasoning to flying fish ... discretely to bring out taste ... and not inordinately to spoil the enjoyment of the diner..." E.L. Cozier: Topic for Today – Barbados Advocate (1987)

"I think his writing encouraged people to view Bajan dialect in a more positive way, and to see local life as something which was a worthy subject for literature." John Gilmore, Association of Literary Writers – 1989

Included with the ten stories within this book is Callender's **Essay on Communication** in which he outlines his thoughts on the equal roles dialect and Standard English should play in the cultural lives of Barbadian and Caribbean people.

Lorna Callender
Realization Studios
2013

Table of Contents

1. A Price to Pay
Do consequences always fit the crime?

2. Dead Man's Hole
Twists of fate and the lessons we learn.

3. Goldsmeller
A smeller of gold?

4. A Farewell
A poignant end after a touching relationship

5. An Honest Thief
Can honesty be mixed with thievery?

6. The Executioner
An occupation that was legal!

7. A Surprise for Agnes
Things are not always what they seem…

8. Up from the Gutter
Does everyone get a second chance?

9. Point of Reversal
No matter how you look at it… creative license!

10. Painting Sold
A snippet of an artist's life

- Essay on Communication: Dialect and Standard English
"Considering how hard the teachers of English Language have worked, I say it is a shame that we are not masters of the English Language…and, simultaneously, confident users of our own speech."
T.C

A Price to Pay

He started from sleep in terror – and leapt up from the ground. For a moment he could not understand the noise, and he crouched there in the shadows with the whites of his eyes large in the darkness. Then he realized that the noise was the barking of dogs, and the shouts of the police. They knew where he was.

The dragnet was closing in. He looked around with a growing panic and a bleak despair knocking at his heart. He was in the shadow of the trees, but ahead of him, where he had to run, the beach stretched long and deserted in the starlight.

He could not remain in the shadows any longer, because, if he did with the men and dogs closing in on him there would be no possible chance of escape.

He stood up for a moment, and then began to run. His feet pounded through the loose powdery sand. He was very tired, because he had already run a long way and had had very little time to rest. Yet, there was no question of stopping, for, around him and coming closer all the time, was the circle of capture, and conviction, and death.

Now, to his left, he saw the first lights of the torches fingering through the trees. He was running closer to the edge of the sea now where the sand was firmer, and he doubled himself over and prayed that the lights would miss him. The trees were intercepting their search and for the moment, he was safe. But now, to his right, where the trees thinned out and disappeared, he saw the dots of light wavering from spot to spot, and he knew that they were coming up from ahead of him also. Behind him, the barking of the dogs sounded even louder. How far behind? Three or four hundred yards? He could not tell.

The only opening was the sea. He thought of this with a sort of surprise that he hadn't thought of it before. Still running, he turned his head and saw the rocks, heard the seething of the water over the long low platform of sharp coral stretching submerged out into the dark. He hesitated, and, as he did so, a torch, clearing the trees, stabbed the darkness over his head and fell upon him, etching him out clearly against the backdrop of the white sea. "Stop!" a voice shouted, and he froze in the glare of the light.

Then he turned, leapt out of the light, and plunged head first under the water, straightening out as quickly so as to avoid disemboweling himself upon the ragged teeth of the reef. The waves surged around him and already his lungs were bursting and his ears were pounding, for he had been almost out of breath when he took the dive.

He came up out of the water behind a rock which shielded him from the glare of the torches and this afforded him a little breathing space. Further out to sea he could discern a large cluster of rocks, and he felt that if he could only reach them, he would be relatively safe. He was gauging the distance towards the rocks, when he heard voices, and he knew that the police were coming out into the sea, walking upon the platform of reef; and, as he looked, light gleamed whitely on the water, and jerked around from rock to rock, trying to spot him.

He took a deep long breath and plunged under the water again. Scraping his knees every now and then he slowly worked his way towards the cluster, averaging his progress by the number of strokes he made. He surfaced again, and a beam of light skimmed over the spot where he had just come up. It was now moving away from him. He dived again. And now he reached one of the rocks that formed the cluster. He reached out and grabbed a sharp jutting portion of it. The in-sweeping wave threw him against it and bruised his body, bloodied his gripping hands, but he did lose his hold. He remained there while fingers of light patterned their search upon the sea and the sky and the rocks, and he shivered from fright and fear that, after all, he might not be able to escape them.

Three thousand dollars, he thought. That was a lot of money. That was the price they'd set on his capture. A lot of people will be looking for me in the hope of getting that, he thought. Three thousand dollars!

He stiffened and looked up. Above the noise of the waves on the rock, he could distinguish men's voices. And now he could hear the scrabbling noise of someone clambering up on the rock. He drew his breath and pressed his back against the jagged side of the rock, waiting, his eyes staring upward. The rock rose behind and above him as he gazed from its base upward to the top edge silhouetted against the dark blue of the sky. He saw a pair of heavy boots, black and sharp against the sky, descending. He held his breath more deeply and his fingers clawed upon the rock behind. There was a splash. The policeman had dropped upon the rock-platform below and staggered as he landed, the light of the torch dancing crazily around at the impact. And then . . . the torch dropped from his hand into the welter of the waves. The policeman was close to him, so close that he could touch him, but the torch was gone, and the policeman couldn't see in the overhanging darkness of the rock.

The policeman swore under his breath, and then shouted "Hi!"

"Hinds?" someone replied.

"Yeah. I loss my light, man."

"Hell, I don't know where he could have gone. I thought I was in front of him. You think he gone back in the opposite direction?"

"He was running this way, man."

"So the smart thing to do is to head the other way as soon as he get in the water..."

"You might be right. Hell, why I ain't think of that before?"

"Hold on. I coming up to you. This place dangerous, man. A man could slip off one o' these rocks and drown easy, easy."

"Well, come up and lewwe go. We going have to wait till morning. We can't do nothing more now."

The policeman scrambled up. The voices receded. The sea pounded on the rock as before. The man waited for a few moments. Then he walked gingerly along the treacherous platform and slipped into the water. In the distance he could see faintly the retreating figures of the policemen. Under cover of the rock, he headed for the shore. He swam warily, for the sharp teeth of the reef were not easy to avoid.

At last he reached the shore. The barking of the dogs had receded into the distance, and he ran along now, all caution gone.

o – o – o – o – o –

"I don't want to have nothing to do with it," his brother said.

"That is your own business. It was only a matter of time before this sort of thing happen. You was a blasted thief all you life, Franklyn, and now you reaping the rewards."

"All right Joe, I is a thief, yes, but that isn't mean I is to get hang for a thing I didn't do...."

"You trying to say you ain't kill her? Man, read the papers. You should see what they saying 'bout you. You up to you neck in trouble this time."

"But Joe, you got to help me. Blood thicker than water. You can't let them get me for a thing I ain't done."

"Look, you may as well stop saying that," his brother said. "Read this."

And he threw a newspaper over to the hunted man, who took it and scanned it with terror-haunted eyes.

The headline said FORDE STILL HUNTED BY POLICE.

It told the world that he had killed a woman, and he had no chance to condemn or save himself.

Franklyn crumpled the paper into a ball, and threw it, in a sudden spasm of frustration, violence and fear, away from him.

"Everybody got Franklyn Forde class up as a murderer," he groaned, "and Joe, I ain't do it. You believe me, Joe, ain't you?"

His eyes searched his brother's face in hope, but Joe's eyes were cold and hard and his lips compressed.

"Listen, you fool," Joe said, and suddenly his expression changed. Tears blurred his eyes, and he wiped them away brusquely.

"We grow up together, and you know how we mother try her best. And you had to turn out so. Time and time again I tell you was to behave yourself, 'cause after all, you is my little brother. But no, you won't listen. And now you running away from a murder charge. And I ain't in no position to help you. The wife in the next room there sick. She sick bad bad. And I been seeing hell lately. The grocery bill over a hundred dollars now and the man say he ain't giving me no more credit. The children hungry. They gone school today without tasting a thing this morning. Look at the old house. Falling apart. I in enough trouble already, and now you can't find nowhere to run but here? You want me to get you out 'o the island. You only out to preserve your own life and you don't care what happen to me once you get 'way. The police can ketch me and lock me up, and it won't matter a dam to you."

"That ain't true, I only asking for a break, Joe. You won't never have to worry 'bout me no more. And you got to understand it is a mistake. I ain't kill nobody. I ain't done nothing to die for."

"You still lying?" Joe suddenly shouted. "You insulting my sense with that stupid lie?"

"I ain't do it." His voice was shrill with the need to be believed if only for a moment. But his brother's face had resumed its former expression. It was like stone.

"I only went into the room to steal, I telling you. I search round and the woman sleeping on the bed. I ain't touch her. And then . . . I hear somebody else come in the room. The woman own husband. I had was to hide. And then *he* stab her. I watch him ... bram, bram, bram, just so ... and she scream out and she husband run. I jump up and run to her. I pull out the knife to see if I could save her, and the blood scatter all over my clothes ... and you never see so much blood ... and then everybody rush in and hold me. I ain't know how I manage to get away. I tell you is the same man got the police hunting me that kill the woman."

"Look, man, you want to get out this island?"

"Yes, yes, yes ...."

"Why you don't tell you own brother the truth then?"

"I tell you I ain't kill nobody... "

His brother suddenly leapt up and struck him. He fell on to the floor. His brother leaned over him and slapped him back and forth across the face.

"Tell me the TRUTH, boy. I want to hear the TRUTH!"

"What I tell you is the truth, Joe," he said trying to keep the panic out of his voice, the panic that kept hammering at his brain. "I ain't kill no woman."

His brother hit him again. And again. He opened his mouth to make another anguished protest, but he saw his brother's eyes, and the denial froze on his lips. "All right, Joe," he sobbed, "I killed her, only I didn't mean to. I kill her. You satisfied? You going give me a break...?"

o – o – o – o – o –

They walked along the beach, their eyes darting from side to side with the fear of discovery in their minds.

"How far the boat-shed is from here?" Franklyn asked.

His brother pointed to an iron-corrugated roof among the trees.

"Is here I keep my boat."

"Other people does use it?"

"Nobody there now. They fishing. I only stay home 'cause Sheila so sick. I wish I had the money to buy the medicine for her..."

"I sorry, man. I wish I had some to give you."

"All these years you t'iefing and yet you poor like me."

"Is life."

"You even worse off now. You is a murderer too."

Franklyn said nothing, but he was full of hurt when he saw his brother look at him that way.

Silence.

And Joe was thinking again: suppose the police come to question me! After all, I am his brother, and the police will surely come. I don't want to get into serious trouble like that. And my wife, perhaps dying and my children starving.

And Franklyn was thinking: What sort of chance I got, with three thousand dollars on my head. Is a wonder nobody ain't recognize me so far.

"This is the shed," Joe said at last.

The boathouse was dark and gloomy inside as they entered.

"The fishing boat there," Joe said. "It old but it can get us where we going. Wait there now till I come back. I got to make everything clear."

"O.K. Joe. Thanks for doing this for me."

Joe didn't answer. He looked at Franklyn for a moment and shook his head slowly.

Then he walked out into the sunlight and down the beaten path that led to the village. After he had gone Franklyn shut the door securely and sat down to await his return.

Joe was gone a long time. When finally Franklyn heard a knock, he was relieved, but cautious. He waited until he heard Joe's voice call "Franklyn!"

Franklyn unbolted the door. And then they were upon him and he went down under a mass of uniforms and clubs, screaming and struggling, as they pinioned his arms and dragged him roughly to his feet.

He snarled like a wild animal, and over the heads of the police in the doorway he saw his brother, his brother who had betrayed him. And, as he strove to get to him, shrieking out curses, someone hit him across the mouth, and they dragged him out into the open, and towards the waiting van.

Dead Man Hole

The cave began near the base of a forty-foot cliff and proceeded for about thirty yards as a narrow tunnel before breaking into a large area as big as a room. Many years before someone had discovered the skeleton of a dead man inside, washed up to the back of the cave and hooked around a rock. Evidently he had been caught by the tide, for when it rose, the water rushed inside, filling the tunnel and the cave, completely covering the hole from outside. When the sea surged, the water sprayed through a tiny pothole some forty yards away from the cliff-top, with the noise like something gargling its throat. And some people said that the ghost of the dead man used to haunt the cliff above the cave.

Parents used to warn their children not to venture into the cave to bathe, but it always held some fascination for the more curious boys. There was a cool, natural pool just before the cave, surrounded by rocks and reefs, and safe from the sea-eggs and congers, and it was here that most of the boys bathed. From the pool looking back towards the land you saw the cave beckoning, and you felt the sudden, frightened urge to go inside and explore. When you were challenged to go inside and you hesitated, you were called a coward and jeered at for the rest of your boyhood life by those who had ventured inside.

One evening two boys came running to the village, naked except for the wet khaki pants in which they had been bathing, and panted out the news that somebody was trapped inside the cave. They had challenged one of the boys to go in and stay for fifteen minutes in the darkness that entered the cave when evening came. They had waited for half an hour and he hadn't returned; but by then the evening was so far gone and the cave so dark that the challengers did not dare to enter themselves. So they raced back to the village, knowing the time was short and that with the night the tide would rise and the sea would come in and cover the hole.

The news spread like lightning through the village.

"Sammy in the hole! Sammy get ketch in the Dead Man Hole and the tide rising!"

People came out of their houses, surprised, worried and wondering. The men in the rumshops sobered up and came outside, their brains befuddled and their eyes blurred, asking over and over again, who it was, how he got into the hole.

"Listen, wunna can't stand there the whole night talking!" a Mr. Rawlins said. "Lewwe go down there and see wha' we could do before it too late!"

Men and women left the village, walked to the cliff and looked over the edge. The cliff bulged halfway down, and the mouth of the cave was on the round curve of the bulge, so that they could partly see the blackness of the cave. They saw that the water had risen from its usual level; that it seemed to come higher almost with every surge of the sea against the cliff.

"Who Sammy it is?" a woman asked.

"Is Clarissa boy. You know Clarissa? She live up by we. Looka she coming now."

Clarissa hurried through the crowd and stood looking down over the cliff, wringing her hands and biting her lips.

"I tell he time and time again not to go playin' 'round that hole, and he won't hear, he won't hear to me at all, and now - wha' he going do? – How we going get he out?"/"The water really rise as high as that?" a man named Errol asked.

"Man it does come three or four foot over the hole. You ain' know how down there stay? It slant down for a little way, then it slant up again. When the water come in, it going right down inside there and filling up the lowest part first. Even if it don't fill up the cave, the longer yuh stan' in there the harder it is to get out. Yuh see, the whole entrance does be under water long before the cave behind get fill up. But the whole thing does get fill up fast fast – tunnel, cave, an' everything – when the tide rising like how it doing now."

"The night closing in fast too."

"Wha' we going do? Anybody got a rope?"

"Nobody ain't think of bringing one? Somebody run fast, and get mine from the boat!"

"Yuh got to get down there before the evening get too dark, hear?"

"Inside there must be dark already, though."

"Who going down?"

The question remained in the air. Nobody answered.

Errol asked again, "Who going down to get the boy?"

And they knew that it couldn't be him, because he could not swim. Now he waited authoritatively for an answer.

The other men looked at one another, and looked away again, at the ground and then at the cliff-edge. The sun edged below the hill on the western side of the village and the sea mumbled, roared and slapped against the cliff, clinging with fingers of foam; fell away and surged forward again. The reefs whitened with the spread of the water over them and the spray flow, blown on the rising wind, was damping the faces and misting the glasses of some of the women standing on the cliff.

"Wait 'til the rope come," Oscar said at last, and suddenly, loudly, and looked from face to face. The crowd breathed out a sigh of relief, but one or two of the men looked at Oscar as if they felt he had shown up their cowardice.

Then a boy came running through the crowd carrying a rope. People seized it in eager hands, tied it around one of the big boulders embedded in the landscape, and threw an end over the cliff. Oscar held it, tested it, and then carefully eased himself over the edge. His feet slipped; he jerked sideways and swung, scraping his back upon the sheer rock wall that fell for about ten feet. He gritted his teeth, his forearm muscles bulged, his vest stretched, his fingers wrapped around the rope. He righted himself, then hand after hand, feet wide apart and flat upon the face of the cliff, he edged his way downward.

The people held their breaths and watched, hoping. The sun dropped below the hill and now only the afterglow of sunset could be seen. The clouds were still lighted, though, and they showed pink on the water, beginning slowly to change to grey as darkness began to crawl across from the east. The sea rumbled and surged and rose.

Now Oscar was halfway down the cliff when fear hit him. The wind blew and the sea came up and slapped the cliff. He felt the pound of its blow and the sting of the spray and he looked down at the angry whiteness below and felt his skin crawl. He closed his eyes and waited for the fear to pass, but his heart was pounding and his back felt cold and his mind was changing. He saw the foam leap to the mouth of the hole and fall inside, and he gripped the rope more tightly and began to return, climbing swiftly back up the cliff, slipping back, clambering on again. He struggled up the last, raised his leg over the edge of the cliff and pulled himself over.

"I – I can't do it!" he gasped. "I can't do it, man. The whole place fulling up by now."

As if in agreement, the water rose and slid down inside the hole, and the sea roared and howled as it slipped away from Dead Man Hole.

The crowd shrank from the spray. They looked at one another and watched as Oscar unwrapped the rope from his fingers and let it fall. They looked at Clarissa, as she sat now crouched against a boulder, biting at her fingernails, wishing and praying. They saw the darkness deepen and the tide come up and they felt something sink inside of them and they began to believe that it was hopeless, that the boy would be drowned inside the Dead Man Hole. And while some edged away, pretending that some inescapable errand back in the village had to be done before nightfall, most of the others remained, fascinated and horrified by the expectation of death.

They turned from watching Oscar walk away, covered with the shame of his defeat, and they decided that it was hopeless, and in their minds they prepared for the funeral next day.

It was then that they saw Bigfoot walking along the cliff. He had just come from fishing; he came in late on evenings. They saw him look towards them and hesitate; then, impelled by the urge to find out the need for the crowd on the cliff, he strode forward. He reached the crowd and they paused to let him in, then fell silent as he gazed down the cliff and saw the Dead Man Hole.

Then one of them giggled. It was inevitable, this giggle at the approach of Bigfoot. He was the village joke, the source of a great deal of amusement, to grown-ups and children alike, in that village. He was a man that eventually had to fall across the peculiar ability of boys for forming nicknames. They had seen him kick a ball once, with such power that it had broken the hands of the man who had ventured to stand in the goalbars on the makeshift field the little boys had formed on the sand.

They had seen him when he ran along the beach with his long strides, carving out a legend for himself and his oversized feet with every step he made. They had marveled at his size fourteen shoes and his inch-long corns. They had named him Bigfoot, and the name had stuck. He was the village idiot; there was no doubt about that.

Bigfoot clumped his feet on the rocky cliff and tuned to face the crowd. He paused, then he spoke. "Wha' happen?" he gruffed out, faintly aware that something was wrong.

Nobody spoke at first; then one person said, "A little boy down there inside the cliff. We trying to save him, but – it ain' look so good."

"Oh," Bigfoot turned away. He didn't care about 'dem li'l boys'; he didn't like them and they didn't like him. They had insulted him for years now, just because of the fact that he had large, embarrassing feet. He felt a hate and a gladness welling up inside his heart. He turned with his rope upon his shoulder and began to stride for home.

Then a heckler in the crowd began to tease. He said, "Bigfoot, where you going?"

Bigfoot turned with anger in his eyes. He saw his challenger standing out before the crowd. He tightened his fingers around his rope and made a sound in his throat.

"How the hell you mean, where I going? Dat is something to do with you" I going home!"

The crowd murmured its shock at his callousness. The mother gave Bigfoot a look of pain and the crywater was running down her face. She went forward to the cliff-edge to look down again, biting at her lips. Suddenly she swayed and someone caught her and led her back to the boulder against which she had been sitting.

"Somebody else try it nuh?" a woman said. - The longer we stay, the more trouble it is! If we don't do it now, it going be too late!"

The crowd saw the truth of her statements. Even then the sea was close to the mouth of the cave. Now with every gush of waves a tongue of water slid over the edge and down, down inside the cave.

"It hopeless," one man said. "If Oscar can't do it, nobody else can' do it. I certainly ain' going down there at this time. In there must be pitch-black and half-full of water by now!"

"Hey – Bigfoot... Why Bigfoot turn back?" somebody asked.

The crowd turned its head and saw Bigfoot striding back towards them, with that angry, challenged look with which he always faced people since the name had fallen on him. He looked down at the sea and up at the sky; then he turned and saw Oscar's rope still tied around the boulder. He stepped forward to it, gripped it and looked down again.

The sea hissed and seethed, rushing among the contorted reefs; little individual waves flung themselves up in tiny peaks and flourished their intent like a dog baring its teeth.

"Stupid little fool!" Bigfoot growled. "Serve he right if he drown. I can't understand why it is these little fools so does get everybody in trouble when they do they foolishness. You ain' know I wish it was <u>all</u> o' wunna down-in there <u>too</u>?"

As he was saying this he was going over the edge. His big feet were wide apart and clamping firmly on the face of the cliff, and he went down fast until he was right over the hole. The sea came up and drenched him in spray and he arched his back as the coldness hit him. Then they saw him go down and disappear inside, and they began to breathe again.

"It all right now. Bigfoot going reach he."

"Yeah… a lot o' water inside there now though. You think he could get to the boy?"

"Why not? The man is a good swimmer, yuh ain' know."

"I know, but that don't mean he could do something that impossible!"

"How you talking so? <u>Why</u> wunna talking so?" a woman said. "Wunna sound like if wunna want - wunna <u>want</u> the boy to dead!"

"Wunna should thank God that Bigfoot still so good as to go down there for the boy in spite o' the way wunna-all does treat he, yuh ain' know!"

"Yuh think he would reach the boy by now?"

"He must be."/"He better come out fast. If it get any darker, he ain't going be able to see a thing. Anybody bring a searchlight?"

"Ronald! Run back to the house and get my searchlight and come, fast!"

"I ain't like how the sea rising. Bigfoot better come outa there fast, yuh ain' know."

The sea was on a level with the lower edge of the hole. Now there was a steady flow of water over the edge. You could faintly hear the sound of water pouring down when the wind and the sea allowed you to. The evening was darkening fast too. Now you had to strain your eyes to see, and the crowd could not help but grow more anxious as the water came up and half-covered the hole and the night closed in, and still the man and the boy did not appear.

And then – the boy did appear. One man turned his head and looked behind him, then shouted: "Sammy! Sammy! What you doing here? That is you for real, Sammy?"

The crowd turned with a peculiar sort of panic, as if they feared that Sammy had joined the dead man's ghost which was said to walk on the cliff.

"Sammy? – Is really he?" Fear nudged at them and they backed away from the boy who was approaching. Clarissa jumped from her sitting position by the boulder and rushed to the boy. Her fear and relief came out in the blows that she rained about his head and shoulders.

"I tell you time and time again not to go down in that hole and still you disobey! I going beat yuh, I going beat yuh like hell!"

"Wait, wait, Clarissa!" Errol shouted. "Lemme talk to the boy." He stepped forward and blocked him from the lashes of his mother.

"Wha' happen, boy? We thought you did drown inside the hole. You mek we send a man down there to get you, and he still down there now. How you manage to get out?"

The boy cringed away, and his face was creased with crying. "Then – them mek me do it!" he sobbed. "They tell me go down inside there!"

"How yuh get out, I ask yuh. Where yuh get up?"

"Through there." He pointed down to his sides and his legs, which were bruised and striated with scratches. "I get cut up real bad, and she beat me!?" He cried at the injustice of it all.

"I did frighten; down there dark and I couldn't get back up when I went down!"

Errol turned away from him. He ran to the edge of the cliff and shouted down to the hole: "Bigfoot! Bigfoot! Come out! The boy up here!" The sea drowned his voice. He shouted again; the wind blew the sound away. He turned to look at the faces of the others.

"What we going do? The man down there searching for he, and he up here."

"He can't get back up outa there now!" A fellow called Jimmy was voicing the thoughts of nearly all of them. "The hole almost full now; he can't get back up!"/"Bigfoot is a good swimmer, man."

"Listen, you know how you would manage to get up outa there? You got to dive down into a little tunnel, and swim down through such a narrow space that yuh could scarcely move yuh hand unless yuh scraping rock. Then yuh got to swim upward to get to the outside. Now, when that place full o' water, yuh would got to hold yuh breath for three minutes or so, considering the problems yuh got down there!"

"Three minutes? Man, it going tek longer than that! You mek it sound easy still."

"I say Bigfoot is a good swimmer."

"Why the hell wunna don't stop sayin' so all the time, you think we ain' know that, man? You does get me vex when I hear you sayin' the same thing over and over so!"

"Tek it easy, man, anxiousness ain' going help."

"Listen, that man going drown!" Jimmy said it as if it were a final pronouncement upon the whole situation. The people heard and secretly they all agreed, although they said nothing to confirm their belief. They sneaked looks at one another and looked away, and they each personally remembered how they had abused Bigfoot in the past. Now Bigfoot had drowned himself, they thought, and for something that he didn't even have to do in the first place, something that nobody had expected him to try.

Then a man shouted, pointing at the spot where the hole was now covered and frothing. The unexpected had happened. They saw, faint now in the darkness, the black spot of Bigfoot's head. They saw him struggle from the hole and fight to escape the backsurge of the rocks. He clung to an outcrop of the cliff and the waves came up and hit him again and again. Then his hands gripped the rope and he was climbing swiftly up. The crowd began to shout its cheers and encouragement as they saw him escape from the heavier breakers and reach halfway up the cliff; then with his big feet spread, toes curling and gripping, he was clambering towards the cliff-top. When he reached there, hands stretched down to pull him over the edge.

They clustered around him, explaining about the boy, asking how he had managed to get out of the hole.

Jimmy was sorry that he had insisted that Bigfoot was going to drown. Now, he, too, wanted an explanation.

"Listen, man, how you hold your breath so? It take a long time to dive outa in there. How you do it?"

Bigfoot looked down upon him, half-amused. Then he called for a cigarette, surprising everybody, for they knew that Bigfoot did not smoke. Jimmy pulled out his pack and offered him one, raised his matches and lit it for him. Bigfoot took one look at it, put it to his lips and with one pull he had dragged it three-quarters of the way. He threw the smouldering butt away, blew out a large, long column of smoke, and said, breathing only slightly more quickly:

"I got lungs, man. I got _good_ lungs; but wunna does only look on a man _outside_. Yeah, my lungs bigger than my foots! Yuh never hear me shout at li'l idiots like he?" He pointed to Sammy and chupsed, then pushed through the crowd and walked away.

Clarissa pushed Sammy forward. "Go 'long, boy, go 'long tell the man thanks! Yuh always interfering wid he, and looka how he was still so good as to try and help yuh! Run and tell he thanks!"

Sammy ran behind Bigfoot's departing figure. "Bigfoot! Bigfoot!" he called. "Bigfoot!"

They were surprised when Bigfoot turned and came after the boy. Sammy stood for a moment, and then he realized the misunderstanding and the danger to himself, and he turned and fled.

The people heard Bigfoot's voice raised in abuse once more, returning relations to normal with every curse that flew from his lips.

"If I catch yuh, I going drown yuh personal myself! Who you think you calling Bigfoot?"

Then he turned away again, and the crowd followed him at a distance. Then one man began to laugh, and others started too, so that, by the time they reached the village, everything was as it had been before, except for the one sure bit of knowledge that there was something to be reckoned with in this man they had been abusing all those years.

Goldsmeller

It was in June 1731, on the 27th, according to the recently found logbook, that the good ship *Virginia* arrived in the Bridgetown roadstead, fresh from Africa, and dropped anchor in Carlisle Bay.

Captain Matthew, the master, was happy as he viewed the many trading vessels in the harbour and the signs of activity in the busy little city, though he was sick and tired. The voyage had been rough, with bad weather and fevers plaguing the travelers, but now they had arrived, and his cargo was safe. The trip would prove worthwhile.

His cargo was thirty Africans, captured or bought on the Niger Delta and brought to the Caribbean to be sold as slaves. All – except one – were healthy and in prime condition; they would fetch a good price in the slave- market next day.

The captain gave orders that the Africans be bathed, fed and generally prepared for the sale the next day. Then he signaled to one of the small lighter-boats that ferried passengers from the ship to the shore, and with his closest officers he went ashore to arrange his business.

"I hope you have good stock?" was the query he most often heard, as he went about advertising his wares.

"All prime young niggers," he answered, "healthy and strong… - except one," he added frankly.

The next day he had his sale, and, the demand being what it was, all the Africans were sold, and very quickly too – except one.

The master dropped the price of this last one to rock-bottom; still he had no takers. He offered to give the fellow away; merchants, planters and freedmen refused his offer. They laughed, in fact, at the idea of owning such a creature as Captain Matthew showed them. Even the others who had just been bought pointed and sneered, and the merchants swore that Captain Matthew was taking them for fools.

"It was a mistake to bring such a miserable specimen to Barbados in the first place," one planter said, and the Captain sadly agreed. It was indeed a mistake; the man had accompanied the group of captives to the ship, since he had a relative among them, and when the ship had set sail, he happened to be on board. They had wondered what to do with him, and there were suggestions to simply toss him overboard; but it turned out that he knew a little English, and was fairly useful as an interpreter (when he was not ill). Still, by this time he seemed to have outlived his usefulness.

The Captain was tired with the whole scene; he and his officers wanted to return to their ship.

Now we all know how terrible, how unjust, how degrading, inhuman and simply *impolite* a business the Slave Trade was. We hate the idea of selling people, I am sure, or of being bought and sold. Undoubtedly; but there is another side to this matter, which I want you to consider.

<u>Not</u> to be bought, <u>not</u> to be sold, was to be in an even worse situation, in those uncharitable times. It meant, to say the least, that something was wrong with you.

For a slave to be bought, in those days, with such a glut on the market, was, in a peculiar way, a compliment to him. It meant that he has passed a test of physical fitness; that he was healthy, strong and fit. No one would want to pay good money for a half-dead slave. No one would want a slave with no teeth, grey hair, and a bent back. Only an idiot would buy a slave with rheumatism, arthritis, bad eyesight, difficulty in hearing and a dry scaly skin.

This African, whom Captain Matthew was – or had been – trying to sell, had all of these characteristics, and more.

To be sold guaranteed this old man a secure life with food, clothing and shelter. Not to be sold was to be exposed to a fate worse than ordinary death; he would perish from slow starvation and exposure to the elements.

You can imagine, then, that some Africans were highly insulted and embarrassed, not to say perturbed, if they were <u>not </u>sold after they arrived in the Caribbean – however they felt <u>before</u> they arrived.

This was the case of that old man, possible the oldest and most debilitated African ever to cross the Middle Passage from Africa to the West Indies.

What could they do with him?

Well, suppose you had brought your <u>yams</u> to market, and sold all except one, and everybody called that one rotten – what would you do? You weren't going to take it back home! You would toss it in the gutter when no one was looking!

And so the Captain and his men abandoned the poor old African man in an alley in the heart of Bridgetown, and hurried away to their ship.

The old man wandered for days and nights around the city. Nobody asked him his name or what he was doing; nobody offered him a piece of bread. Rain soaked him, sun burned him, and people walked around him, there where he lay at the side of the street, too weak to move, after the fifth day of his enforced freedom.

This fifth day was a Sunday, the Lord's Day, and an old Protestant preacher passed by. He was to deliver a sermon that night, and was meditating on the parable of the Good Samaritan, when he found the starving old man. He had, in fact, passed him by on the other side, when his conscience smote him mightily. Like Saul on his way to Damascus, he stood transfixed in the light of this revelation. What good was preaching about the Good Samaritan if he couldn't act like one?"

And so he took the old man, and bound up his wounds, and poured in oil (but no wine), and set him on his own horse, and took him home.

Well, the preacher's wife wasn't too pleased. You know how it is with some wives when their husbands come home suddenly with an unexpected guest. But the preacher – John Reynolds, Esquire, was his name – soon persuaded her to accommodate the old man.

"But we don't want a slave!" the lady cried.

"My dear, he is not a slave. He is free!" John Reynolds said.

"He is good for nothing," said Mrs. Reynolds, uncharitably.

"He must be good for <u>something</u>," replied Mr. Reynolds, charitably but uncertainly.

"Yes; me good for something," the old African suddenly said, surprising them.

"So you know English!" exclaimed the preacher. "At least, a form of it. What is your name?"

"In my own language they call me a name that means, '**Smeller of Gold**'."

"A very fanciful name!" marveled John Reynolds. "And what can you do?"

"That is what I do."

"What? – What is it that you do?"

"Smell gold. I can find gold for you."

"Impossible!" said the preacher and his wife together.

But two days later, when he was stronger, Goldsmeller went out in the morning and returned at midday with three lumps of gold.

"Where did you get these?" John Reynolds asked, astounded.

"They come from inside the earth. I can find more."

The preacher looked down at the lumps of gold. They were enough to build a church. He was glad for them, but he had a terrible fear that in the long run there would be much trouble.

"Never, never, <u>never</u> you do this again!" he shouted at the surprised old man.

"All right," the African said, and he was deeply puzzled, for he had assumed that all Englishmen liked gold and would do anything to lay their hands on some.

The African kept quiet after that. But truth, like a whale, will surface. The histories do not say, though some scholars suspect, that it was the preacher's wife who spread the tale. Suffice to know that in one week, all over the island, this was the news: *that there was a man who could find gold by his nose, the way a dog could find bones.*

Now, as we know, the world is full of dishonest people.

The master of Lowdown Plantation was such a one. He was also one of the richest men on the island, but he wanted still more wealth. When he heard of this old man with the wonderful gift for smelling gold, he wanted to get hold of him immediately.

Quickly he summoned two of his strongest slaves, Achilles and Hector, and told them to get some digging implements and bring his carriage and horses. Then accompanied by Achilles and Hector, he hustled away to the compound of John Reynolds, and without much effort he captured Goldsmeller and took him away.

He was surprised when he saw the old man, for it was he who had first suggested to Captain Matthew, that day of the slave-market, that the old man should be dumped like garbage

"Take the carriage to the West Coast of St. James!" the planter ordered Achilles. He had a plan. At Jamestown, also known as the Hole of Holetown, there was the river-mouth where the first English settlers had landed. Persistent rumour had it that pirates of old had landed there, too, and buried their treasure-chests in the soft earth at the mouth of the river.

Well, the planter thought, he would get Goldsmeller to find a treasure-chest or two. He was going to be even richer

It wasn't the best weather for that sort of enterprise. Since the early morning of that day, the atmosphere was abnormally still, and the heat was steady and oppressive. Far to the east, thick clouds gathered, and lightning flickered among them. Not a whisper of long leaves came from the sugar-cane fields. Cattle huddled together in motionless groups, forming circles with their heads together, lowering their horns; and chickens clustered on perches, hiding their heads in their wings. Any fool could see that a hurricane was approaching.

The historians say that the great hurricane of 1731 was one of the worst that ever hit the island.

Perhaps the master of Lowdown Plantation noticed these things; perhaps he was concentrating on the thought of finding gold. They were now in Holetown, by the River which gave the town that name. The residents, fearing the storm, stayed in their houses, and the streets were deserted. The four men left the carriage and proceeded through the trees on the beach. The sunset was ominous; the trees stood breathless and tense.

The old man, roped like a dog on a leash, sniffed at the air and the ground. He could smell trouble as well as gold, but, he reflected, he had lived a long life.

"Right, use your nose, find some gold!" the planter ordered.

"All right, sir," mumbled the old man.

Now I have heard of dowsers and diviners, of forked rods dipping and pendulums swinging, in efforts to locate gold; but Goldsmeller's nose, the legends say, outdid all of these.

"Dig here," the old man said, stopping and pointing.

Achilles and Hector unslung their spades. They were standing on the mud-flats on the southern side of the river, close to the water, and it was easy to dig.

They struck gold just as the hurricane broke.

A steady blast of wind and rain swooped down from the sky and plastered the island all at once. Tree branches tossed their leaves away and broke in half; the surface of the sea turned white with froth. Coconuts flew from trees, were tossed bouncing along the ground by the mighty wind, and already there was the sound of houses breaking apart and people screaming.

Soaked in rain, wild as the hurricane itself, the madman of Lowdown Plantation kept shouting to his slaves. "Dig! We still have time!"

"No!" shouted Goldsmeller. "We must leave at once. I can smell danger."

"Dig!" shouted the planter again.

Above the stridor of his voice there came there came a terrible and dreadful sound that paralysed them all. A low rumbling shook the ground. Goldsmeller pointed up the darkened river-course, too frightened to speak.

The others turned, and gasped at what they saw. They tried to run, but, as in a dream, their feet could scarcely move.

An avalanche of water came down the river course, sweeping everything away in its path. It hit the four men, drowning their screams, and took them out and away, past the river mouth and out into the open sea.

Two days after the hurricane they found the old man washed up on the shore, barely alive. There three Lowdown men were never seen again.

Mr. John Reynolds took Goldsmeller home again, and nursed him back to health. But the old man was never the same again. The hurricane had given him a cold, and stopped his smelling forever. His gold-smelling power was gone.

"Perhaps it's all for the best," Mr. Reynolds said.

And no doubt he was right.

A Farewell

There was a sort of finality about everything. The day was Old Year's Day, the period that of sunset; the end of a day and a year, and also the end of a young man's first phase of life. And at the same time, there was a beginning; for a new day and a new year lay ahead, and new opportunities were in the distance too. At this moment, everything was perfectly still, though, as if this period was the point at which both aspects, that of a past, and that of a future life, merged.

There was that hushed and perfect stoppage of all moving things... the sun hung still in the melted tints of the sky, and the colours of fading evening and approaching night had met and blended in a perfect pattern... the tints of the sea and the sky were the same, so much so that one could not discern the line where the sea ended and the sky began.

The jetty stretched long and narrow out into the sea, its great posts stiffly standing in the water like black sentinels, silhouetted against the orange-tinted surface of the water. The sea itself was calm and peaceful; there were scarcely any waves, but the whole surface of the water was rising and falling. It seemed as if the sea were breathing in its rest.

The jetty was deserted except for the lonely old man who sat at its end with his legs dangling over the water, watching the sea. His back was bent and his head was half bowed, as if the unseen weight of age was tangibly pressing down upon him. His clothes hung in tatters about his body, and the white hair of his bare and weathered head was long and straggling. I felt sorry for the old man in his loneliness; but I knew that he was happy just to come and sit there on the jetty evening after evening and watch the smouldering sky, and feel the dying sun's smile on his face.

From the time I was a small boy, I would many an evening wander out on the jetty and see the old man sitting there. He would smile his little twisted smile at me, and beckon me with his withered hand, calling me to sit beside him. And I would go and sit with him on the boards of the jetty, with my feet dangling over the edge, and with his protecting arm around me, and we would talk together.

He would tell me about his boyhood days, and of his early life ... how, at sixteen years of age, he had run away from home and gone to sea in order to escape from his strict Puritanical parents ... of the adventures and escapades he had had. And I would listen rapt to all he had said, and wished that I could live a life like his.

He had a way of suddenly breaking off the conversation and remaining lost in dreamy recollection of some specially cherished and poignant memory. I remember the way I would gaze into his clear and un-aged brown eyes as he stared ahead of him, but not at the sea or anything visible at all ... it was at some personal, invisible scene re-reeled upon the memory tapes of his mind ...

Mom and Dad, with their strict religious ideas and their deep prejudices of anyone whom they regarded as below their status in society, hated me to talk with the old man, and more than once they told me to keep away from him. But he exercised a hold, a fascination over me, and I felt some profound link with him, and so, in spite and because all they said, I constantly disobeyed them and went and talked with the lonely old man.

Mom said, "Listen, my boy, besides being undignified to speak on such intimate terms with a man of his sort, it is definitely low-minded. You must remember your position. It is mystery to me what you and he could have in common to talk so long and so deeply about. And then, it is highly embarrassing to us that you should so blatantly refuse to fraternise with the boys of your age and social standing, and the sons of respectable neighbours, and go and talk with that old man. People are beginning to feel that we allow and condone it. I wonder, what exactly *do* the neighbours think!"

That was typical of her. She never did anything unless she first satisfied herself that the neighbours would think nothing less of her for doing it. And Dad never did or said anything of himself except what Mom expected and demanded of him. I often wondered why I was so radically different from them ...

In rebellion I continued to 'fraternise' with the old man... in spite of the fact that he dressed in rags and went barefooted and lived in the dismal remains of an old shack, and in spite of the fact that I was always well groomed and cleanly dressed, with shoes on my feet and with expensive watch and ring.

When I was accepted into High School Mom told me that I would now have to bread my links with the old man. "You can't allow the people to see you in your decent , school clothes conversing with that man," she said. "I don't know why you are always encouraging that man around you ..."

"You don't have to know...," I muttered.

She was shocked for a moment and then she said, coldly, "You see, association with that man has already corrupted you. You never would have been so disrespectful to me before."

"I thought you were always right then," I said. "I didn't have my own ideas then."

"But the ones you're having now are going to lead you astray," she returned. "You will turn out bad like any other self-willed fellow, and in spite of all the good training we gave you."

"I don't see anything wrong with the old man," I said stubbornly. "It's just that you can't see any other point of view but your own, and that is not my fault."

My retort left her speechless, and I walked away and went through the front door immediately.

I knew that she was watching me but I did not care, and I walked down the avenue between the rows of quiet bungalows, crossed the main road, and went out on the jetty. It was still early and the old man had not yet arrived, but I sat and waited for him. And all the time I knew that she was looking through the dining-room window and watching me, but I did not care.

When the old man heard that I had made the grade to High School he was pleased. I could see that he was fighting for words to convey his feelings; and in the end he failed to find those words. But I got more satisfaction out of the few sentences he uttered than from all Mom and Dad had said.

He looked at me and said, joy lighting his deep eyes, "My son, I am real glad to hear that. I know that you going make the best of your opportunity, and become somebody really worthwhile. God bless your future."

And so I went to High School and managed to struggle through my exams successfully, finally leaving with a satisfactory amount of Ordinary and Advanced

Level certificates. Mom and Dad were satisfied, and Mom, not so much thinking of my future, but more to gratify her own desire for prestige, I felt, demanded that I go to a university.

I had not seen the old man for some time and now I hastened down to the jetty to talk to him, happy that I had lived up to the standard expected of me.

He heard my footsteps and felt their vibration through the boards of the jetty, and turned his head to see me coming. "You do not have to tell me," he said and his face creased into a smile. "I can see you have good news. You have done well, I know, son."

I dropped down beside him on the jetty, and dangled my shoes over its edge. "Yes I have," I said. "I have. I have."

The old man was silent for a little time, gazing into the sunset with his steady clear gaze. His face was coloured with the vivid splashes of the smouldering sky, and some of the red light glinted on the tears that had gathered in his eyes.

"I am glad, my son, I am glad." That was all he said.

After a pause I said, "Mom wants me to go to a university. What do you think?"

"What does it matter what I think? It will not change anything. I realise, although you have not told me anything, that she doesn't like to see us talking ... because I am too low for you ..."

I was silent. There was no point in pretending that it wasn't true ... The old man knew that he had embarrassed me and he continued quickly, not taking his eyes from the sunset; "Of course you got to go. Your

Mom is paving the way for you to become a responsible, respectable man..."

"But it is not my desire to go. I shall miss this place, this life, you, and everything I have enjoyed for so long a time ... I hate the idea."

"It is not time for sentiment," the old man said. "You have your young life to live, whilst I have only to die. I have enjoyed your company, and I would hate to see you go, but it would be selfish and unfair of me to tell you not to go away and study ..."

"Okay," I had said. "I will go."

But it turned out that I did not have to leave the island after all. A local university had come into being, and I went there. Mom would have preferred to boast that I was at an English university, but she had to be satisfied to boast that I was at the local one. And I was happy to remain in the island and continue my way of life.

It was during my final year at the university that a neighbour – not a very great friend of mine – informed me that Mom and Dad were not my true parents. I had been adopted by them when Mom was told she would not be able to bear any children of her own. I had mentioned this to the old man, but he had been singularly uncommunicative. All he would say was, "Ask them, son. They have been good to you. Ask them."

Later, I asked Mom and Dad about it and demanded to know the truth.

"That old man, damn him, has been telling you things," she countered angrily. But when I gave her the source of my information, she told me the story was true; I have been taken from a poor married couple who could not afford to support even their only child; and I had been reared in a middle-class society. Mom and Dad had tried to make me into *their* child, and to make me feel and think like them and to kill the instinctive affinity I felt towards the lower-classes.

I had tried my best to find out who my parents were, but there had been no clue to help me. Even the old man failed me here.

And now I had become a man. I had gained my B.A. degree. And I was called to take a post in another land, and would soon be leaving this island.

I went to see the old man on the jetty. He gazed into the sunset and talked softly to me.

"So you are going away, my son," he said. "Well, God bless you, and may your future be a bright one."

"Thank you, old friend," I said, placing my hand on his shoulder.

"You must be twenty by now," he said.

"Twenty-one on the 31st December. The same day I have to leave the island."

"Going to take up a new life on a new year, eh?"

"That's it."

He felt into his pocket with his right hand, and then he pressed something into my hand. I glanced down and saw it was a fifty-cent piece.

"Now look, old man ..."

He motioned me to be silent. "I know what you going say. But that to you is a symbol. I cannot help you, with money or otherwise, but I want you to take it along so as to feel that you have my support and fellowship in all that you do, my son."

Touched, I drew off my ring and slipped it upon a wrinkled finger of his left hand. "Goodbye, for now, my friend," I said gently. "But I will see you and tell you goodbye just before I leave for the airport, on Old Year's Day."

He nodded, and turned to look into the sunset once more, and I walked off the jetty.

And now the day of my departure had come and I was ready to leave for the airport.

I got out of the car and walked along the jetty in the fading evening light. As usual, he was sitting on the jetty, his face turned towards the red sky and sinking sun. That strange sense of finality filled my mind ... the world was perfectly still. And I walked to tell him goodbye.

With that goodbye, I intended to ask the question which I had long pondered. For I had begun to suspect that the old man was more than just a friend to me. By dint of judicious questioning, of the old man's neighbours, I had learnt that he had had a son who had been adopted, and that he had hidden the fact from for so long because he felt that I would disappointed and ashamed to learn that he was my father ...

My footsteps pounded on the jetty, but this time the old man did not turn his head. He still gazed at the purple sea and sky, unconscious of my approach. I felt a sudden pang of deep sorrow, in knowing that this was the last time I would walk down this jetty and see the old man sitting at the end. For in the next few hours, I would be flying through the night sky bound for new lands and a new existence ...

I reached the old man. "Good evening, old friend," I said, standing behind him. And he did not seem to hear me, but still stared across the sea. And the whole world was waiting and expectant ... the sun hung still, and the sea whispered warningly to me.

"Good evening, Father."

No answer, no movement ... I grasped his shoulders, suddenly realising that this goodbye was indeed final, and pulled him over backward. His limbs were still supple and the sun's rays had warmed his body, but the old man was no longer breathing ... His clear eyes were open and glinting in the sunset light, and they held a message for me, as had had his lips with their twisted, quizzical smile. I could not ask the question any more, but I knew the answer. The smile told me.

An Honest Thief

Every village has a 'bad man' of its own, and St. Victoria Village was no exception. It has Mr. Spencer. Mr. Spencer was a real 'bad man', and not even Big Joe would venture to cross his path. Besides, everybody knew that Mr. Spencer had a gun, and they knew he had used it once or twice too. Mr. Spencer didn't ever go out of his way to interfere with anybody, but everybody knew what happened to anybody who was foolish enough to interfere with Mr. Spencer. Mr. Spencer had a reputation.

Now at the time I am speaking of, every morning when Mr. Spencer got up, he made the sign of the cross, went and cleaned his teeth, and then left the house and went into the open yard to look at his banana tree. He had a lovely banana tree. Its trunk was beautiful and long and graceful, the leaves wide and shiny, and, in the morning, with the dew-drops glinting silver on them, it seemed like something to worship – at least Mr. Spencer thought so.

Mr. Spencer's wife used to say to him, "Eh, but Selwyn, you like you bewitch or something. Every morning as God send I see you out there looking up in that banana tree. What happen? Is you woman or something? Don't tell me you starting to go dotish."

And Mr. Spencer would say, "Look, woman, mind you own business, eh?" And if she was near him, she would collect a clout around her head too.

So one morning Mrs. Spencer got vexed and said: "You going to have to choose between me and that blasted banana tree."

"Okay, you kin pack up and go as soon as you please," Mr. Spencer said.

So Mrs. Spencer went home to her mother. But, all said and done, Mrs. Spencer really loved her husband, so after two days she came back and begged for forgiveness.

Mr. Spencer said: "Good. You have learn your lesson. You know now just where you stand."

"Yes, Selwyn," Mrs. Spencer said.

"That is a good banana tree, and when you eat them, you will be glad I take such good care of the tree."

"Yes, Selwyn," she said.

The banana tree thrived under Mr. Spencer's care.

Its bunch of bananas grew and grew, and became bigger and lovelier every day. Mr. Spencer said: "They kin win first prize at any agricultural exhibition, you know, Ellie."

"Yes, Selwyn," she said.

And now, every morning Mr. Spencer would jump out of bed the moment he woke and run outside to look at his banana tree. He would feel the bunch of bananas and murmur, "Yes, they really coming good. I going give them a few more days." And he would say this every day.

Monday morning he touched them and smiled and said: "They really coming good. I going give them couple days more." Tuesday morning he smiled and said, "A couple days more. They really coming good." Wednesday morning – and so on, and so on, and so on.

The lovelier the bananas grew, the more Mrs. Spencer heard of them, all through the day. Mr. Spencer would get up from his breakfast and say: "I wonder if that tree all right! Ellie, you think so? Look, you better go and give it a little water with the hose." Or he would wake up in the middle of the night, and rouse his wife and say, "Hey, but Ellie, I wonder if the night temperature ain't too cold for the tree! Look, you best had warm some water and put it to the roots ... along with some manure. Go 'long right now!"

And Mrs. Spencer would have to obey.

One morning Mr. Spencer came in from the yard and said as usual, "EEllie, girl, them bananas real lovely now. I think I going pick them in couple days' time."

"Always 'couple days'," she said, peeved. "Man, why you don't pick them now quick before you lose them or something? Ot no paling round the yard. You ain't got no paling round the yard. Suppose somebody come in here one o' these nights and t'ief them?"

"T'ief which?" Mr. Spencer said. "T'ief which? T'ief which?"

The truth was, nobody in the village would have dared to steal Mr. Spencer's bananas, for, as I have mentioned, he was a 'bad man'.

Then, one day, another 'bad man' came to live in the village. He was the biggest and toughest man anybody had ever seen. He had long hairy arms and a big square head and a wide mouth and his name was Bulldog.

Everybody said, "One of these days Bulldog and Mr. Spencer going clash. Two bad men can't live in the same village." And they told Mr. Spencer, "Bulldog will beat you!"

"Beat who? Beat who? Beat who?" Mr. Spencer said. He always repeated everything three times when he was indignant.

And Bulldog said: "Who this Spencer is? Show him to me."

So one evening they took Bulldog out by Mr. Spencer's, and he came up where Mr. Spencer was watering his tree and said:

"You is this Mr. Spencer?"
"How that get your business?" Mr. Spencer asked.
"Well, this is how. If you is this Spencer man, I kin beat you." Bulldog always came straight to the point.
"Who say so? Who say so? Who say so?"
"I say so."
"And may I ask who the hell you is?" Mr. Spencer asked. "Where you come from?"
"You never hear 'bout me? Bulldog said, surprised. "Read any newspaper that print since 1950, and you will see that I always getting convicted for wounding with intent. I is a master at wounding with

intent. I would wound you with intent as soon as I look at you. You wants to taste my hand?"

Mr. Spencer didn't want to, however. He looked Bulldog up and down and said:

"Well, I ain't denying you might stand up to me for a few minutes." He paused for a moment, and then said: "But I bet you ain't got a banana tree like mine."

He had Bulldog there. It was true that Bulldog had a banana tree. But beside Mr. Spencer's it was a little warped relic of a banana tree.

Bulldog said: "Man, you got me there fir truth."

"That ain't nothing," Mr. Spencer said. "Look up there at them bananas."

Bulldog looked. His eyes and mouth opened wide. He rubbed his eyes. He asked: "Wait – them is real bananas?"

"Um-hum," Mr. Spencer replied modestly. "Of course they still a bit young, so if they seem a little small…"
"Small!" Bulldog said. "Man, them is the biggest bananas I ever see in my whole life. Lemme taste one."

"One o' which? One o' which? One o' which?"

Bulldog didn't like this. "Look, if you get too pow'ful with me, I bet you loss the whole dam bunch."

"Me and you going get in the ropes over them same bananas," Mr. St. Spencer said. "I kin see that.

And now get out o' my yard before I wound you with intent and with this same very chopper I got here."

Bulldog left. But he vowed to taste one of Mr. Spencer's bananas if it was the last thing he ever did.

Mrs. Spencer told her husband: "Don't go and bring yourself in any trouble with that jail-bird. Give he a banana and settle it."

"Not for hell," Mr. Spencer said. "If he want trouble, he come to the right place. Lemme ketch him 'round that banana tree. I waiting for he."
"C'dear, pick the bananas and eat them all quick 'fore he come back and t'ief them."
"No," Mr. Spencer said. "I waiting for he. I waiting. Let him come and touch one – just one, and see what he get."

A few days passed. Bulldog had tried to forge Mr. Spencer's bananas, but he couldn't put them out of his mind. He did everything he could to rid his thoughts of that big beautiful bunch of bananas which had tempted him that day in Mr. Spencer's yard.

And then he began to dream about them. He talked about them in his sleep. He began to lose weight. And every day when he passed by Mr. Spencer's land, he would see Mr. Spencer watering the banana tree, or manuring it, or just looking at it, and the bananas would seem to wink at Bulldog and challenge him to come and touch one of them.

One morning Bulldog woke up and said: "I can't stand it no longer. I got to have one o' Spencer's bananas today by the hook or by the crook. I will go and ax him right now." He got up and went by Mr. Spencer.

Mr. Spencer was in the yard feeling the bananas. He was saying to himself: "Boy, these looking real good. I going to pick them tomorrow."

Bulldog stood up at the edge of Mr. Spencer's land: he didn't want to offend him by trespassing. He called out: "Mr. Spencer, please, give me one of your bananas."

Mr. Spencer turned round and saw him. He said: "Look, get out o' my sight before I go and do something ignorant."

And Bulldog said: "This is you last chance. If I don't get a banana now, you losing the whole bunch, you hear?"

"But look at ... But look at ... But look at ... Mr. Spencer was so made he could scarcely talk.

Now Bulldog was a conscientious thief. He had certain moral scruples. He liked to give his victims a fifty-fifty chance. He said: "I going t'ief you bananas tonight, Spencer. Don't say I ain't tell you."

"You's a idiot?" Mr. Spencer called back. "Why you don't come? I got a rifle and I will clap a shot in the seat o' you pants, so help me."
"Anyhow, I going t'ief you bananas," Bulldog said. "I can't resist it no more."
"Come as soon as you ready, but anything you get you kin tek."

"That is okay," Bulldog said. "I tekking all o' them."

Mr. Spencer pointed to a sign under the banana tree. It read:

TRESPASSERS WILL BE PERSECUTED.

"And for you, persecuting mean shooting." Bulldog said nothing more but went home.

A little later in the day, a little boy brought a message on a piece of note-paper to Mr. Spencer. It read, "I will thief your bananas between 6'oclock tonite and 2 o'clock tomorra morning." Mr. Spencer went inside and cleaned his gun.

Mrs. Spencer said, "But look how two big men going kill theyself over a bunch o' bananas! Why you don't go and pick them bananas now and mek sure he can't get them?"

"Woman," Mr. Spencer replied, this is a matter of principle. I refuse to tek the easy way out. Bulldog is a blasted robber and he must be stopped, and I, Adolphus Selwyn McKenzie Hezekiah Spencer, is the onliest man to do it. Now, you go and boil some black coffee for me. I will have to drink it and keep awake tonight if I is to stand up for law and order.

At six o'clock Mr. Spencer sat down at his backdoor with his rifle propped upon the step and trained on the banana tree. He kept his eyes fixed there for the slightest sign of movement, and didn't even blink. It was a lovely moonlight night. "if he think I mekking sport, let him come, let him come, let him come."

Seven, eight, nine, ten, eleven, twelve o'clock. And no sign of Bulldog. And Mr. Spencer hadn't taken his eyes off the banana tree once. In the moonlight the tree stood there lovely and still, and the bananas glistened. Mr. Spencer said, "They real good now. I going pick them tomorrow without fail."

Mrs. Spencer said: "Look, Selwyn, come lewwe go to bed. The man ain't a fool. He ain't coming."

"Ain't two o'clock yet," Mr. Spencer said.

And all the time Mrs. Spencer kept him supplied with bread and black coffee. He took his food with one hand and disposed of it without ever taking his eyes off the tree. The other hand he kept on the gun, one finger on the trigger. He was determined not to take his eyes off that tree.

One o'clock. No Bulldog.

Half past one. No Bulldog.

Quarter to two. No Bulldog.

Mrs. Spencer said: "The man ain't coming. Lewwe go to bed. Is a quarter to two now."

"We may as well wait till two and done now," Mr. Spencer said.

Ten to two. .No Bulldog.

"Hell! This is a waste o' good time," Mr. Spencer said.

Five to two.

At one minute to two, Mr. Spencer looked at his wristwatch to make sure and turned his head to his wife, "But look how this dam vagabond make we waste we good time."

Then he looked back at the banana tree. He stared. His mouth opened wide. The banana tree stood there empty, and the only indication that it had once proudly displayed its prize bunch of bananas was the little stream of juice that was dribbling down the bare broken stem.

The Executioner

They often looked at the man and wondered what his thoughts were. They knew his profession well; he was the hangman at the island's Central Prison.

At first, when he was new to the job, he had been questioned several times by acquaintances and friends – how did it feel to be responsible for so many deaths? They asked, though perhaps in more modified language, in keeping with the friendship they professed. He had explained that <u>he</u> was not responsible; he was carrying out an order; it was a command given to him which he obeyed and which resulted in the death of murderers.

Later, though they did not lose interest, they asked no more questions. It seemed that he, or they, had changed their ways. He was certain that the change was partly his, at least – for now he remembered his earlier faltering with a grim laugh. He no longer felt the tremendous emptiness in his solar plexus that transfixed him, and once or twice had made him almost faint, and he no longer tried to learn about the man he was to kill, where he lived, what his family was like. He no longer tried to apologise telepathically to the victim that the state (not he) was going to execute. However gentle he might feel, his task was not affected; the rope still seemed most ungentle to the man fluttering at its end.

Later, he withstood every impulse to find out anything about the man to be killed. He had read the murder trials avidly before; now he restrained himself from thinking or reading about what went on in the Courts and the Prisons. And, as the number of his jobs increased, as he got more experienced, more skilful, indeed, he did them in freedom. In fact, had he noticed it, he saw himself as carrying a tremendous power; however ostracized he was because of it. He wielded death, and in a righteous manner. No one had the right to kill someone else, he told himself. Anybody who kills somebody else should suffer execution.

He tried, too, to think that the Courts were infallibly just about every conviction; for this seemed essential to him at one time, if he were to proceed into his job with a clear conscience. But he had been shaken once or twice, when he used to take interest in trials, and rather than challenge the justice of the island's laws and their administration, he stayed away from newspapers, courts, and arguments. He was notified when he had a job to do; he arrived, he efficiently did his job, and returned home to his wife and family.

For he had a wife and two children. It had seemed to amuse and amaze some people at first, and they had been apt to wield her marriage as a weapon against his beautiful wife: the women especially, for they noticed how their men watched her body as she walked on the street. He, too, had been suspicious of her at first, doubting her motives for seeming so attracted to him after they had met a few times, wondering if she really could be interested in him, if she was after money; if she knew what he did for a living. Time, and plenteous loving, had solved that problem; now he felt secure with her, grateful for her and the normality she brought to his life; happy with his son and daughter. And making money, too. They owned a modern bungalow and he was amassing some comforts; he was paying hire-purchase dues on a number of household appliances.

And yet all this could be disturbed, all this sense of well-being punctured, when somebody was bold enough to make comments; this usually happening after he met someone and the talk turned to jobs. At first he used to say, "I work at the prison", but now he said, "I am the Public Executioner" and watched people's eyes for reaction. Many people were not bold enough to comment; a few laughed, pretending or believing it was a joke; the sensible ones (he thought), seemed embarrassed. Three or four times, in his fifteen years of this work, people were genuinely curious, unbiased, honestly trying to put themselves in his profession, to imagine how it would feel to actually stop a person from living – and in full knowledge and approval of the community at large

One man had said, "Man has a delight in watching other people die. Most would not admit it, but most of us would kill somebody if we were sure that there is no form of recompense awaiting, in this life or afterwards. But it is fear that keeps people from killing one another. Once, people killed in order to survive. So you, my man, you have the greatest job in existence!"

He had pondered that, had searched out that daring, uncomfortable thought. For his admirer was saying that he should enjoy his job, for the joy of it, and see himself as a boon to mankind. At first he had not dared to think it; now more and more, with every verbal conflict he had, he became hardened into the philosophy of that clever character. He developed an exterior that made men cower; he was always aware that they saw death around him, saw a miasma of last thoughts, of pain, of hate, of murderous spirits cleft from the bodies of their hosts and seeking revenge upon the executioner.

The executioner had no friends. He was very polite and made no social errors, for people filled with dislike and/or fear spring into offensive or defensive action most suddenly. He lived well within the law, and was well versed in litigation. One thing was sure, he always told himself, he would never commit murder. He had seen too many men die; he had dreamt of being hanged; he had passed through many a psychic journey in what it must be like. When he envisaged himself hanging, he was devastated with terror. He kept himself well in check, therefore, when he talked to people, he refused to listen to words that would anger him; he was conscious that they felt that life was nothing to him, and therefore he would kill quickly. When he knew their thoughts, and brooded upon them, he sometimes got so angry that he kept alone, meditated on them in solitary places, eased his mind and came back to his job.

That is why, this night, he was sorry that he had left home. It was not usually so; usually, on Friday nights, he came to Simpson's rumshop and drank for a couple of hours, arriving home after midnight, and not sober enough to be quiet. Still, not too drunk, for you never could tell who bad minded man, bent on revenge for some executed brother or son, would be lurking in the canefields. But he carried a gun, and people suspected it too, and he had never been molested on his lonely Friday night walks back home to his loving wife and children.

Now, in spite of his immediate rage, he felt that recurring gratitude for his wife. It was she who had made him recover from a numbing psychological disturbance; she had made him human in spite of all the populace did to label him the opposite. Other human contacts were brief and laden with suspicion; with her he could be free, could live a normal life, and raise their children.

Intermittent with this thought and its concomitant desire which made him hasten towards his home, was the blind rage which had overtaken him back there in the rumshop. It had made him leave the company of the drinking comrades who, in their alcoholic frankness, had commented freely on his chosen field, coupled with jokes about undertakers and gravediggers and, yes, scavengers; and had he not left them, his defensive anger would have come into action.

It was a bitter exchange between him and them, and, finally, he hoped – aloud and fervently, so sincerely that the words fell like a curse upon them – that someday he would get them in the right position; he was waiting for the chance to loose the trapdoor on some of them; and he could even give police information that bound to put one or two of them, or their relatives, right into his hands.

He had hurriedly left after that, as they recoiled from his words; and now the words kept hammering back to him, forcing him to see the scene and the impact on them; making him consider the <u>truth</u> of such words, wrung from so deep inside his being. He felt he had gone too far; he shouldn't have said that; he shouldn't have let himself hear himself uttering those words; the rum infused the sincerity of the statement with dreadful accuracy. He swallowed his self-exposure with despair, made more agonizing by the fact that he had ignored and locked away his deepest motives. It was this: **he loved to kill**. And with the thought of the legality of his act of execution, came the thought that perhaps he did it that way because it was the only way… because he was too cowardly to commit any act that led to the gallows? He remembered brave men hanging, some whom he knew were innocent; once it was his cousin – and a friend of his had barely escaped his hand; some died cursing, totally unafraid, immune from any self-doubt even when they felt the immediacy of the noose.

He arrived at the door of his house. He checked his thoughts, made an effort to push aside the gloomy perceptions tugging at his mind, and entered the house. He entered quietly, expecting that Marion was sleeping. He thought of lovemaking and his heartbeat quickened. Usually, on Friday nights he would be in no condition for loving after all that rum; and when he arrived home, she would be too deep into sleep anyway. Now, tonight, he was early, and semi-sober. He crossed the drawing room silently, walked past the bedroom when the children would be sleeping, and entered their room.

He heard the gasps and quick breathing even before he turned the light on and was shocked by what he thought incredible.

His wife sat up in bed, her face distorted with fright, and her companion scrabbled up and off the bed, standing upright, naked, pressed against the wall, already knowing that he could not escape.

It came to the husband's mind immediately that the young man was not to live. The decision was as irrevocable as the knowledge that from that point onward, he could never trust humanity again. It seemed conclusive proof of all he had lived for.

He fumbled the gun out of his coat pocket, and felt a peculiar freedom as he lifted it and blasted three shots into the boy.

It was no repetition of a familiar act, no busman's holiday; a perverse kind of fulfillment entered his mind as the realization came: he had done it of his own free will, and without being on duty.

His wife said nothing. She watched him hypnotized.

He left her still there kneeling on the bed; walked out of the room, out of the house.

He headed for the police station. Even if he felt like fleeing, there was hardly any point to that. He was well known; and the Island was so small that there was scarcely anywhere that you could hide.

The trial was short and swift; and the sentence was obvious to all long before the formalities were done.

Then, one morning soon after, the people gathered on the little slope east of the prison, murmuring among themselves, wondering at the strange coincidence that had come about. The time crawled towards six o'clock, and the deathly silence descended.

The new hangman was young and nervous. For the first time in his adult life, within his half-empty mind, the condemned man felt like crying as he looked at his successor and imagined what his future would be like. The young man misunderstood, and became more apprehensive. His agonized look was cut off by the cap-blindfold pulled over his predecessor's eyes.

The young man watched him as he stood on the trapdoor waiting and both were wondering what would happen next and what it would be like.

A Surprise for Agnes!

"Josephine, come here. I want to talk to you," the old woman said. "I is your grandmother, and I want to hear the truth from you right now."

Josephine didn't answer.

"Girl, you hear me talking to you? You feel that you too big to be controlled by me?" the grandmother said. "Come outside here at once, and let me hear how come you get into such a situation."

It was as if the grandmother was talking to herself. The bedroom door remained closed, and not a sound came from behind.

"Listen girl, it look like you want me to put my hand 'pon you. You playing that you don't know me yet? You think you's a big woman now, eh? This is why you behaving so? Well, as long as you inside my house you have to conduct yourself in a certain way, and right now you going have to explain yourself to me."

There was silence again. Then came Josephine's voice; "You could say what you like, I ain't care."

The tone of the voice made the grandmother pause for a while. She shook her head slowly from side to side, then she raised the hem of her skirt and wiped at her eyes.

"Lord have mercy," she said: "Look what she come to now, Josephine, how you could let down you father and mother so? What I going to tell them when them come home and find you with a bastard-child?"

"Them could do what them like, too," Josephine declared. "When is the last time you see them? What I know 'bout them? I ain't see them since I have been four years old. Think they care 'bout you or me? They could do what them like, yes."

"But looka this ungrateful, wussless nigger-woman," the grandmother said.

"I ain't no worse than you," Josephine said. "How come you is my grandmother? You never get married all you life. Is just that children follow whatever they elders does do.

The grandmother began to cry. She couldn't understand how Josephine could have turned out so, after all the good training she had had as a child growing up.

"Your parents left me in charge of you," old Agnes went on, after she had stopped sobbing and could talk again. "I feed, I clothe you, I do my best to keep you at school so you could take in a little education and make something outa youself. I try hard to bring you up in the right way, carrying you to church with me, sending you to Sunday School; and everything that I think was good for you, I try to do. But no. From the time you reach a certain age, all you interested in is acting like you is a big woman, and now yuh sins ketch up with you."

"You behaving like I's the first and the last one to bring home a child," Josephine said.

"I going put you outa this house if you can't talk no different, you hear?" Old Agnes was getting hot now, she didn't intend to put up with that kinda talk no longer. "So help my Christ, you ain't going stand in here another day unless you tell me who is the man that put you in that condition. You hear what I say girl? You's a big woman, right? You carrying baby. And if you's a big woman you should have a big man looking after you.

You going have to leave inside this place, and find the man that put you so."

Josephine didn't answer. The grandmother pressed her advantage.

"Every day as God send, Lord you know…I try my best with this girl. I do everything that was humanly possible to keep she 'pon the right path. I did love this child with all my heart; I did intend to leave everything for she when I dead. But Lord, you know she ain' deserve none of it now. Looka the shame and disgrace she bring down 'pon all the family. What you parents going say when I write and tell them? How you think they going feel?" The grandmother began to cry again. "They can't blame me for what you gone and do; I try my best, I couldn't do nothing more. I try to stop you from talking to all them young men. I explain everything 'bout manhood and womanhood to you. I teach you the things that you oughta did know. I never expect that you woulda turned out so low-minded and bad. Josephine, you ain't feel sorry for what you do? How you think I feel this morning? How you think your parents going to feel? And what the church-people going say?"

"Church-people?"

"Is that 'pon you mind, right?" Josephine answered back. "I know it all the time, too. It ain't nothing to do with how you feel 'bout me. Is only them damn church-people you can think 'bout, and you own personal embarrassment. I did know all the time….. you ain't care 'bout me, you only want to clear yourself of all the blame."

"Wha' kinda onreasonable idiot you is?" the grandmother asked. "Wait, you bewitched, girl? Is I to be blamed for you wussless behavior? I know where you went to get yuhself so? I know the dirty places that you does put yuhself in? I know the men you does meet? Girl, I going put my hand 'pon you, here? You giving me cause to lick you down, and if I start 'pon yuh, yuh going think is the Devil heself."

"Won' be the first time I think so." Josephine muttered.

"Well, well, well," the grandmother said, "I never expect it, that is all I can say. And you a big member of the church too…how you feel?"

Josephine didn't answer.

"You is a member of the Choir," Old Agnes said, "And you is a Sunday School teacher. You is also a Group Leader and a Local Preacher. Everybody was admiring you and saying how you so nice and Christian. I ain't know how to face them now. They going to be hurt deep deep. And especially Reverned Samuels."

"What he have to do with it? Josephine said. "You think he is God?"

"What he have to do with it?" the grandmother repeated. "Girl, you is a real fool for truth! You can't even see how you lose out 'pon all you chances? Reverend Samuels was you only chance in life, girl, in a little island like this, I usid was to pray to the Lord and ask He to look kindly 'pon you and send along a nice husband for you. When I see how the Reverend did admire you I was hoping that one o' these days he woulda choose you for he wife. Yes, that is what I had in mind for you, nothing less. And he did like you too. How you going face he now? What you going say?"

There was silence again. When Agnes listened carefully, she could hear Josephine crying inside the room.

Ten minutes passed while the old woman sat and pondered. Then she nodded slowly. She knew what she had to do.

"Yes, I going have to expose you," she said. "I going have to wash my hands clean of you, and clear myself before the church-people and the Lord. I ain't going take the blame for the way you turn out. Is tonight self I going to church, and after that I going bring the Reverend home here to have a word with you personal. You don't respect nothing I say, but you going listen to him, you going to have to tell him something, cause you have a high respect for him – at least, yuh had it."

Josephine didn't answer.

"You could stand inside there drawing-up like a sick fowl the whole day," the grandmother pressed on. "So help me, I going put you in the hands of the church, and I want to know how you going feel, sitting down 'pon the back bench with you belly high in the air. It shameful, it shameful…girl, that is all I can say to you."

Josephine remained in the bedroom all day. When Agnes entered she turned her face to the wall, lying in the bed.

At seven o'clock, Agnes said, "Listen, I going to church now." Josephine didn't answer.

Agnes left the room, took up her Bible and Hymnbook from the centre-table in the drawing-room, went through the front door; and Josephine heard her walking away, her high-heeled boots beating the pavement.

Josephine sat up in bed. But she glanced down at her belly and wondered how her grandmother knew that she was pregnant – there was no visible sign, she thought, her stomach didn't indicate it yet.

"These old women does know by just looking at you," she said to herself. She rubbed her hand over her belly. She wasn't certain what she would do. She knew she wanted to get out of the house as soon possible, that she couldn't live around her grandmother like this, because every day it would only be noise and quarrelling. Whatever happened, she wasn't going to stay.

Josephine got out of bed and went into the kitchen. She made a cup of tea and sat drinking it and thinking about the situation; wondering how her grandmother would take the truth when she heard.

Reverend Samuels, she thought, Huh. She wanta bring Reverend Samuels to talk to me. She laughed aloud, and her voice contained a note of bitterness.

Reverend Samuels, she thought. A nice young preacher, from England. Well liked and admired by all in the island – everybody wanted their granddaughter married to him; everybody was sending their daughters and granddaughters to church.

Reverend Samuels doing very well, she thought. I is the fool and Agnes, and all the rest o' them. Wait 'til she find out who it is put me so.

Choir practice, indeed!

Up From the Gutter

When late evening came he stopped digging and stretched. He wiped his face and walked over to the plum tree where his shirt hung; took it off the limb, put it on, beat his heavy fork against the tree to dislodge the dirt clinging there, left it by the tree and walked out of the field and up the road

He whistled as he walked. This was the first day on the job, and it had been a good day. He hadn't had a job for a long time, and now that he'd got this one he was determined to keep it. He didn't intend to fall back into the old way of life, the way of life he had decided to reject only that day. He wanted desperately to change, to keep himself and his household, to help Margery in her efforts to pull him up from the gutter and make him somebody respectable.

It was only that morning that he had thought of turning over a new leaf. Maybe it was only because Margery had treated him so callously. She had refused to open the door when he came home and he had to spend the night sleeping under the house. He had lain there and thought for a long time. Then he decided that so far his life was rotten, but there was still a chance for him to change it. He should have made more of an effort to deserve the good that Margery had done for him, he told himself. She had found him down and out, had fed him, clothed him... married him. The house, the furniture, everything was hers and he possessed nothing at all. At least he could have been grateful. But no.

He did not care to work; remained at home all day, drank if he had the money, read the comics in the papers, slept most of the time. Margery slaved and never complained at all - at least, not about his laziness. But she had been wild last night. One thing she would not tolerate was his seeing other women. He never saw anything like her fits of temper when she thought for the slightest reason, sometimes for no reason at all, that he'd gone to see another woman. She would sulk for days and days. She would drop savage remarks to him, usually about her trying all the time to make him into somebody, reminding him all the time that she'd taken him and pulled him up out of the gutter; that, had not for her, he would still be there. She could have married someone else, she said; but no, she'd gone and stuck herself with him in the hope that she could do something for him. Now she was not sure.

He seemed to hear her voice then, ringing in his ears. She talked like this all the time when she got angry. But last night was the first time things had gone so far; she had refused to open the door.

The rain had come down and the water formed little streams that ran and soaked him where he lay. He awoke in the dark and cold, shivered as he squatted by the limestone pillars that made the foundation of the house, and wished for morning. Remorse had stung him deeply.

"This is ignorance, man, bare ignorance. I shouldn't be in this position no more. Is my fault, too. I ain't doing as well as I can; Margery right. Another night like this and I going dead too. My health ain' the best anyhow; I ain' a well man."

His plight had made him think for a long time, and as he gritted his teeth against the draughts, and tears formed in his eyes, he kept planning, there where he was, in the foreday morning, underneath the house

"As soon as light come I going get up and go and look for a job. I got to show Margery that I change... and

I also got to do something 'bout this Ursula; I can't let she mash-up my life like this. I going take back that money I get from she, and tell she that everything done. I been taking advantage of she too."

So that morning he got up and crawled from under the house, and knocked at the kitchen-door to get in; but Margery wouldn't open the door. He heard her moving around inside the house and he called to her, but she would not answer. She was still very angry at him, he realized; and she had a good cause this time.

The evening before, she had seen him coming out of Ursula Boyce's house. He had ducked back, out of sight, but it was too late, and when, after walking about for a long time, he ventured to go home, the house was shut up tight, and call as he might, Margery refused to open the door. Now he hadn't seen her since yesterday evening. He wanted to go home and tell her that he had changed, that he had a job, and that from now on she could be proud of him. He really wanted to tell her that, to make her feel better, though he knew his own weaknesses.

But he couldn't go home yet. He had to return to Ursula's place and give her back the fifty dollars she had given him. Yesterday he had been only too glad to take it; he had intended to gamble with it, though he'd told her that he wanted it for a down-payment on a bicycle. Now he didn't feel like keeping it anymore. Besides, he was afraid that Carlo would find out. The money really belonged to him, and he was Ursula's. And it seemed as if Carlo could be just as furious and vindictive as Margery could be when it came to this matter of unfaithfulness.

So instead of going home immediately he turned off the road and went to Ursula's place. He knocked, waited, called; but she was not at home. He put his hand over the door, slipped the latch and went inside; opened the bedroom door and looked around familiarly, wondering where she was. Then he saw her handbag on the chest of drawers. Good. He'd put the money in her handbag and she should know where it came from. If not, he could easily tell her the next time he saw her. And at the same time he would tell her that he was through with secretly meeting her; that he was sticking to Margery, that their affair was over, and that he was reformed. He closed the door and walked away, hoping that it was really the end of his relationship with Ursula. Now he would go home and face Margery with his apology and his wish for a better life in the future.

He saw the rainclouds gather as he walked down the road towards the village, and he began to hurry. Already the evidence of coming rain had given the evening a premature darkness, and he wanted to be safely home when the rain came, for he saw that when it began it would continue through the night. He reached the village, hurried through the street and reached the house. He paused, then went to the front door and knocked, apprehensive at the thought of facing his wife; but the house was closed too tightly for anyone to be at home.

"She ain't home?...Uh wonder where she could be….she must be gone at the shop…Margery! Margery!" he called; and only the silence answered.

Now curious faces looked out at neighbouring windows, and he wondered why. He descended the steps, turned to face the next-door neighbour who was looking out of her window, and asked:

"Where Margery?"

The woman hesitated, then she said: "Margery gone 'way from the house. She pack up and left this morning 'bout eleven o'clock. It look like she left for good, too; a lorry come and take 'way the stove, the furniture and everything."

Shock staggered his mind. He stared disbelievingly at the house, at the woman, and muttered an oath. Margery was gone. The house was empty and he couldn't even get inside for the night.

He didn't know what to do. Search for her now? But no, the night had almost come and it would rain bucket-a-drop tonight. He had to wait until tomorrow before he could begin enquiring after her. But there was nowhere to sleep tonight; that thought was uppermost in his mind.

He muttered thanks to the woman and walked quickly away from the stares of the other people.

Where was he going?/He could find somewhere to sleep, man; he'd been out throughout the night before, when he didn't have anywhere to live. He would sleep on the steps of some shop, or walk about for the whole night. But the rain was coming, and it looked like a heavy downpour. He didn't relish the thought of spending another cold, lonely night; but he didn't have a choice.

A rumshop – that was where he would go first. He needed a couple of drinks. After that he would go and find somewhere to sleep; tomorrow he would enquire to find where Margery had gone.

He walked back the way he had come; saw an open shop and went into it, still thinking of his problems.

"But she shouldn't leave me like that though man. She shoulda give me a chance to explain myself, man. She left in so much hurry; like she had it planned..." The thought struck him, penetrated his logic as if it had been waiting there all the time.

How could she leave so easily? Did she – could she – another man?" Jealousy flared within him and spread, swift as a canefire, before he checked his thoughts.

No, she could not have done that... she would not do that, he told himself. And, still pondering, he went and leaned on the bar, beckoned to the bartender, and call for a rum.

Outside, the night closed in and the rain began to drizzle.

Now it was dark. The rain had increased. The time had crawled to ten o'clock, and the last rumshops were closing. There was no one on the streets. He was alone, and the rain continued to beat heavily, steadily down. He was soaked through, and cold, and very drunk, and he had nowhere to go, nowhere to sleep.

He walked uncertainly down the road. The streetlamps seemed to dissolve in sparkling tears in the heavy rain. The road had slimed over, and the water gushed along the narrow gutters, cascaded and roared in the ones beneath the road. A dark shape scuttled past his feet, and another. Rats! They were deserting the gutter, coming up through the iron gratings covering the holes in the pavement, heading for higher ground. They scuttled past him in the flooded road, some of them squeaking in fear. There movements were erratic, their direction uncertain; and as he watched them bundle together or jump here and there to escape the fast running water, numbly he understood their terror. The world was wet tonight. Rain kept on hissing down, and thunder rolled far up in the darkness, among the invisible clouds. He hadn't seen a night like this for a long long time.

He found another half-closed rumshop and staggered into it. Four men huddled around a domino table looked up and saw him enter, dripping wet; shot glances at each other and stopped playing just for a moment. He looked at them; they looked at him. He swayed, weaved over to the bar, and ordered rum.

The man behind the bar said, "Too late man. I done selling for the night. Why you don' go home, man? You ain' got nowhere to live? This bar closing right now, so you can't stay here, if that is what you thinking!"

He stared at the bartender and muttered something; turned and walked over to the man at the domino table. They sat still when he approached, dominoes still clutched in their hands.

One of them said, "Move 'way, man. Move 'way. We ain' want you here."

He stood still, swaying slightly, looking at them, water running from his body, his shoes muddying the floor. He mumbled, "All right man, I kin find somewhere else to go ... other people..." and turned away, lurching a little, searching for the door.

A man got up from a bench in a corner where he had been sitting alone, and came to him. He held his shoulders and steadied him, guided him to the door, and came outside into the dismal night with him.

"You ain' hear wha' happen?" the man asked. "Nuh man?"

"Who is this – Oswald?"

"Yes, is me. You ain' hear wha' happen?"

"Wha' you talking 'bout – Wha' happen?" he said, squinting to look into Oswald's face.

"Carlo find out, man" the fellow said. "Carlo was just in here. He find out 'bout you and Ursula, man. He say how she give you all his money, and how you and she treat him like he was a fool. He vex, man; he feel everybody laughing at him. He beat Ursula bad, and she in hospital now. It happen this evening."

"Man, you lie, man!" he said, when he understood.

"Is the <u>truth</u>! Carlo was in here not too long ago – the police ain't find him yet. And – he looking for you. That's what I come to tell you, man. <u>Carlo looking for you</u>!"

"He ain' understand! I done wid that. I is a – changed man."

"You could change?" asked Oscar, and eyed him strangely.

"Man yes. I ..."

But Oswald had turned away and re-entered the shop, and he was alone once more, with the rain hissing all around him and the squeaking, half-drowned rats hurrying past him, crazy with fear.

Suddenly he too was frightened, because he remembered that Carlo wasn't too good in the head. "What he want with me? <u>What</u> Carlo want with me?"

Alone in the darkness and the cold and the rain, he walked through the blur of streets and houses, and he was very drunk. Now he scarcely thought of Margery, or of the next day; thought only of some high, comparatively dry shop-step on which he could wait out the night. He staggered down a dark road, down another;

past closed, sleeping houses, lightning ripping across the sky, thunder shaking the world. He splashed through the rising, swirling water on the road, stumbled, faltered, righted himself and swayed on. He tottered for a long time through the relentless rain, and then he was too tired to go any more. He wanted to get out of it, to find somewhere to sleep, somewhere where Carlo wouldn't find him...

He thought: Carlo wouldn't be searching for me on a night like tonight. Carlo himself running from the police and - he ain't got no time for me."

He remembered Ursula, and hoped she wouldn't die.

"She better not!" he said aloud. "That would make Carlo a <u>murderer!</u> And then, if <u>I</u> involve in it, Margery could never come back! Ursula better not go and dead!... But I wonder where Margery is now. Wherever she is, she safe from the rain, and she warm... I wanta see she, tell she that things change, things going be different. Wanta tell Carlo that too, and Ursula. How come I change and I ain' get a chance to tell nobody?" he wondered suddenly. "How come they ain' <u>notice</u>?"

He stopped and gazed downward at his cold, bedraggled frame. Maybe they didn't notice, indeed. He looked the same way. Just as mean, calculating and roguish. His features, his gait and his voice were the same. The nimbleness of his hands, his former-pick-pocket activities... these were still foremost in people's minds. To them, he still deserved his hated, nine-year-old nickname, a name he hated as forcibly as he had deserved its application.

"And now, I is still a drunkard too. But I going change. All I want is for this night to pass...that is all...for this night to pass."

Then he saw what would be the most suitable stopping-place for the night – the high step of a shop with a low overhang of roof, which would protect him from some of the rain. He knew he wouldn't be able to sleep, that he would sit and shiver most of the time; but he could go no farther, there was nothing left to do.

He turned away from the middle of the road and headed towards it; stepped over the rushing water in the gutter and was about to go up the step when he heard the voice shouting his hated name.

The name seemed to mix with the thunder and the hiss of the rain, seemed to enlarge until it beat at the clouds themselves, so suddenly, so dreadfully, did it enter his senses.

Then:

"I coming for you!"

It was Carlo.

He wished he could run, but he was tired, oh so – tired!... The alcohol had turned his knees to rubber.

"Yes, I coming! You know why, too! Where my money? You think I ain' know 'bout you and <u>Ursula</u>?

He opened his mouth to say something. Rain streamed down his face, into his dilated eyes. His brain was blurred; his tongue was heavy inside his mouth.

Now Carlo was right there in front of him, looming like a tower. Lightning seared across the sky, in a flash etching the anger on Carlo's face, the white of his teeth as he snarled; the cold white sparkle of the icepick in his hand.

He tried to say something to Carlo – that he was sorry, that things would be different, that he would leave

Ursula alone – but … only muttered, the drink muddling his tongue.

Carlo shouted once more: "Ursula <u>dead</u>, you know that? Ursula dead, and is <u>you</u> that cause me to kill her, Rat! You Rat!"

Then he stabbed.

The name penetrated as deeply as Carlo's icepick. But strangely, there was no pain, just a curious, frightening numbness. He sagged down into the gutter, muttering stupidly. Carlo turned and ran away into the darkness, leaving him there.

He began to cry; tears mingled with the rain on his face.

"No chance to live a good life now…no more…" he muttered to himself; and died.

Point of Reversal

When they stopped running they were on the waterfront. They leaned, all four of them, against the wall gasping for breath. Only Rupert's gasps were different. Something was wrong with him. When he moved his hand from his chest they saw that he was stabbed.

Mackie examined the stab, squinting his eyes, jutting his head forward, knife still in his hand. "Oh my Christ, it look bad." The others crowded Rupert, Edward supporting him with an arm beneath his armpits, and they looked at the wound. Rupert's hand drooped, his knees buckled and he was moaning something, his eyes half-closed.

"What we going do?"

"I ain't know. I ain't realise..."

"We got to get help." Ivan was always looked to for an answer. "We got to take him home. Who know where he live?"

"I know the area, but I ain't know the house."

"Christ, look at the blood. A chest stag is a bad thing, man."

"Let we move him, out of the light. Anybody could see we here."

"Rupert? You could move?"

Rupert was now sagging on the wall. His hand unclenched. His knife clattered to the ground. Mackie picked it up, closed it, closed his own, briefly seeing the blood at the tip, snapping it shut and slipping it in his pocket. "Let we move him round here."

They half-dragged him and put him in a sitting position against the wall in the dark. His head fell forward. He was still groaning and trying to stop the blood, but it was coming fast.

"We wasting a lot o' time." Ivan's glance shot around at the faces. "Lissen, what we going do?"

"The Memorial Hospital ain't far. Let we leave him. Is the best place."

"We got to get a car then. Mackie, you go." Mackie slipped out of the darkness and hurried up the road along the waterfront.

Edward bent to Rupert, held his head upright. "Rupert. Rupert, look at me. We going take you to the hospital." He looked carefully at his face, but it was empty and quiet. "Rupert. Listen. Now you ain't going tell them nothing, not even your own name, hear?"

Rupert coughed. Edward looked up. Ivan was looking at him. They didn't like how he coughed.

"If I had a good chance... "Edward said. "I woulda fix the son of a bitch. I would fix him good."

"We ain't know he had a knife. In future we got to watch these people for knife and gun."

"It happen so fast. All I know is, I see you take his wallet. And just so, a knife inside he hand."

"I think Mackie catch him."

"Yeah, but only slight."

"Too much people was around the place. If we did have only a little more time... but that damn woman scream."

"We got to watch things. We nearly get catch that time. They wouldn'ta taken me though. I woulda dead first, and take some of them with me. Nobody ain't putting me in no jail."

"No, no point fighting all o' them. We ain't want to kill nobody unless it necessary."

"Hey, but what happen to Mackie? He taking very long ... he sin't know we got to hurry, look how Rupert bleeding."

"Look, this must be him right now. Yeah. He coming."

A car drove up and stopped. A door slammed. Mackie hurried back to them.

"Let we go, fast. I think they spot me getting it just now."

"My God, everything wrong tonight. You realise Rupert going be in hospital for a long time now?"

Is the first thing I think about. And they going to ask him how it happen every day. Come, lift he, nuh."

Mackie was at the feet and Edward at the head and they lifted him, walked to the car and laid him out on the back seat. He wasn't groaning much now, but the breath was funny inside his chest. Mackie felt the urge to drive real fast.

The three sat in front and Mackie started and pulled with a jerk from the kerb.

"Rupert won't talk, man." Ivan turned to look at him. "I know Rupert good good ... Rupert?"

"No, don't shake him, man. That don't help."

"Rupert? Lissen good. Now you ain't to say nothing to none o' them people – who you is, what happen, nothing. You ain't even know us." He could see

Rupert's eyes, white in the semi-darkness of the car. "He understand"

"You sure it all right then."

"What else we can do? It look serious to me; we can't take him home. And the hospital close to here. After we leave him there we free from trouble..."

"Get ready to lift him out." Mackie had already reached the hospital, now he swung into the entrance. He drove towards the doors of the building. A taxi was there but no one was about. Ivan and Edward leapt out of the car, pulled the back door open, lifted Rupert and placed him on the steps. Then they ran to the car again, got in, and Mackie drove away.

"They bound to find him there in a few minutes."

"Yeah."

"You think he going be all right?"

"What you worrying 'bout, man?"

"You see the amount 'o blood in the back seat?"

"What the ass, man, Rupert ain't going dead.

"Listen, where you think is a good spot to get rid of this car?"

They found a young man stretched out straight on the top step of the entrance to the hospital building. His eyes were open and his mouth twisted in pain and his hands were clasped over the spot that was the source of the red that covered his white shirt. Some orderlies rushed out with a stretcher and they lifted him onto it and rushed inside again. They always worked like that. But there was no real need for it now, because the young man was dead.

O – o – o – 0

When the late bus stopped at the terminus, only one woman got off. She was young. She had a handbag and as she walked away into a darkened street she glanced from side to side and gripped it tight. It was Friday night and she had twenty five dollars pay. Thieves came out especially on Friday nights, and they took everything you had, no matter how poor you were. There were some who would rape, too. Lately the crime rate had increased. And if that worthless man had any consideration for she, he woulda have the sense and decency to wait for she and walk she home from the bus stop. But he wasn't no blasted good at all. She worked so damn hard for both of them, he scarcely ever got a job, and why the hell she decided to live with he in the first place, she was only a fool. Anyhow, as soon as something happen she, can always go back to she Ma...

She walked and reached the little house where she lived. (... And look the damn man ain' even at home again, what he expect this is, every night I going sit down frightened in this house? Suppose somebody attack me one o' these nights, one o' them gangs that going around molesting people... Rupert, one o' these days you going come home and look for me and you ain't going find me at all, you ain' going ever see me again, you watch and see.)

She opened the door, stepped inside, closed the door and locked it, switched the light on. A cockroach tried to escape but she put her foot on it. She went straight into the bedroom and took her clothes off. She hung them up carefully, slipped on a nightgown and lay down on the bed. She clasped her hands between her legs and thought of Rupert, and she was still peeved, but she wished that he was there in the bed beside her, she would have liked that then.

After a time she fell asleep and when she woke it was half past six in the morning and she was still alone in the bed, Rupert hadn't come home.

What the hell, what happen now? That selfish, inconsiderate brute getting worse every damn day...

$$O-o-o-0$$

He would have done anything to stop her from finding out. But that was impossible as soon as the police and the newsmen knew. It would be the final break. Things had been going badly between them for a long time now, and the scandal of this would be the end.

It made him a little angry. He felt wronged, almost; as if she should accept it without any fuss. After all, he had been good to her, in his own way. And he'd tried to be good to her in *that* other way too. But it wasn't right for either of them. She'd only suspected it before; her friend had hinted it, goddam that woman; but now all the confirmation would be there. She had only to hear the name of the club and she would know.

That worried him; and he was still shaken by the events of last night. He squeezed his eyes shut and shook his head, opened them and stared at the roof. Why it have to be him? So many rooms in the building, and they choose his to enter.

They came in the middle of the act too. He jerked his head around and they were there, one laughing, all the others viciously angry at the insult to their manhood... Bloody stinking auntie-men. Look at the two of them. Two big stinking *men!*" One of them was reaching for his clothes, searching the pockets of his pants. He had seventy dollars in there.

He looked from side to side. The three others were by the bed; Jerry was cowering under the sheet whimpering like a child. The men were laughing. One said, when he saw him staring around, "You don't think 'bout nothing, man. You remain right there in bed with you girlfriend."

He kept still. He didn't have a weapon.

Then he saw Jerry's hand going under the pillow, Jerry's eyes pleading with him to look away; he turned, backing Jerry, hearing the men talking excitedly over the money. Felt Jerry fumbling for his hand – what the hell, not *now*. Felt the knife thrust inside.

Their attention had been distracted, but they saw him coming. The one closest to him was clawing his back pocket, the others had flicked knives. They rushed at him. He felt the knife enter somebody. Then one raked across his chest. He sprang back, took to the wall, dropping the knife, watching them approach...

"We should kill you. We should cut out your ..."

"Hey, lewwe go man, leave him, come" one shouted. Jerry had begun to scream and footsteps were running toward the room. The men turned and ran, scrambled through the window and fled...

The proprietor called the police. Fool. He could have hushed the thing. No need for them to come in…

And there would be investigations and maybe trials and all the publicity...he hoped they wouldn't find the men,,, That would be hell for him,,,

The radio said: "A thief who was stabbed in the chest by one of his victims in a knife duel at the Small

World Club last night, died in the Stanford Memorial Hospital soon after... So far he has been unidentified."

"Last night the police were called to the Club where Mr. Michael Dufy of Flat River, St. James, made a report. Mr. Dufy said that ..."

Oh Christ, it start, he thought. He switched off the radio and closed his eyes.

Painting Sold

"Yes, I like it. I'll take this one," the man said, after a long pause. He stepped back and half-closed his eyes, nodded slowly. "I like the way you paint. I've always admired paintings with that kind of touch—you know, thick, powerful brush-strokes, strong colour, rough texture. You've been painting a long time now, evidently."

"Yeah, a long time now." The artist reclined in his armchair and looked up at the painting on the wall. He had sensed that his visitor would choose that one, from the beginning. The man had said that the face was an attractive one; he was struck with it from the time he saw it, though he did not know why. Then he had stood in the middle of the narrow little room and viewed the rest from there. His eye had come back to that painting time and time again. And he wanted to buy it. The artist was glad that the man wanted to buy one. He needed money. He felt that he was lucky to have met this man. It had happened just by chance; he had hitch-hiked a lift and they had started talking, then he had mentioned that he was an artist, and the man had said that he would like to see his paintings. So he brought him to his room and showed him the ones he had hung there. The visitor liked his style. He wanted to buy the portrait of the Chinese girl.

The artist looked at the painting, and he was sorry that it had to be the one chosen. He liked it too, and he knew that he would miss it, but he couldn't afford to let the sale slip through his fingers. He hadn't sold a painting for a long time.

The visitor looked at the painting, and the artist looked at the visitor. He wasn't sure, but he felt that he knew this man. He watched his face carefully, straining to ascertain whether or not he was—what was the name? Norman. Michael Norman. But he didn't ask. He just sat watching his visitor while his visitor watched the painting. And he became sure that this was Michael Norman.

"How much do you want for it?" the man asked. The artist said, "A hundred and seventy five."

The visitor hesitated. Then he looked around the room again, his eye quickly taking it all in. The rough bed and dirty sheets. The easel and the oils and the old dry tubes of paint. The single creaking armchair, the half-empty wardrobe, the pile of books on the floor. The cabinet in the corner and the little stove. He said, "Okay," and took out his wallet, opened it, counted off some notes.

The artist watched him and knew that he was affluent. He scratched his beard, got up, took the money, threw it on the table among the paints, and went and took the painting down. He looked at it for the last time, remembering the time he'd painted it, recollecting the brushwork and the composition and the difficulties he had encountered in painting it. He looked at the face with a wry expression, and handed the picture to the man.

He said, "Sorry I can't wrap it - I ain' have any paper."

"That is all right, man." The visitor buttoned his jacket and slipped the painting under his arm. "Thanks very much. Good night." He walked towards the door and the artist followed, said goodnight and watched him walking down the steps. Then he shut the door and returned to his armchair and listened as the car started and the man drove away.

The artist felt in his pocket for a cigarette; he had none. He found part of an unfinished one on the floor, and he lit it and pulled on it, looking up at the space on the wall where the picture had been. It was dark with dust, and the space was void. But he sat looking at the wall as if the picture was still there, and he began to reminisce.

It was a year after he had left home, and he was hard up. He had thought that he could have managed on his own, but he wasn't any better off. He became depressed. His exhibitions had been poorly attended, and scarcely anybody bought his paintings. Here, as everywhere else, society had official favourites; his name was unknown. He took jobs, but never for long, and he painted and brooded and smoke and drank. Sometimes he thought of returning to his island, to his home, but pride held him back, even if his parents would accept him again. But he knew that they would not; he had drifted too far away from them, and they had washed their hands clean of him and consigned him to the Devil.

And he knew that he could never stand the atmosphere of his parents' home again. Narrow-mindedness and fanatical religiousity. They had desperately tried to make him conform to their way of thinking, to kill his ambition to be an artist and stifle his creative powers. He had kicked out against it until he could stand it no longer, and he had left with the optimistic hope of his success as an artist that the last years had dissipated.

One night he went to a dance. They were celebrating the opening of a new art gallery, the largest in the island. It was a big occasion, held at the Hilton. He sat and watched the couples on the open-air dance floor, and he smoked and thought and drank.

That was the night he met Alison Chen. He saw her face first. It was an arresting face, and he kept looking at it, watching her across the table, trying to memorize her features to reproduce them when he returned home. He had never seen Chinese features quite like these. She noticed he was watching her and she hesitated a smile; and asked him why. He told her, and then they had discussed Jamaican painting for a long time. She was willing to pose, she said, and he gave her his address and told her to drop in anytime.

They danced. Byron Lee and the Dragonaires played, he remembered, and their music was beautiful. So were the lights, and the sky, and the mountains in the distance, stark against the glow emanating from the sinking moon.

It was one of those atmospheres where you feel as if you were holding eternity in an hour and you said an eternity of things. He didn't say anything. He just noticed the lank black hair and the curve of the eyebrows and the forehead and the nose and the little mouth and the structure of the skull beneath the skin and the pressure of her fingers on his back. And when she talked, she asked him about himself and he told her about his painting and his wish to be a success and why he had left home, and that he thought he was a failure after all. People saying that he had promise and that he should work harder and he would succeed, and all the time his knowing that he could go no further because a former something was lacking in his work and he had stopped being original and creative a long time ago.

Some days later she came to his room and stood in the middle of it as his last visitor had done, and said how beautiful his paintings were and how much she liked his style. And she bought some of them. After that, she came again and they talked some more; soon he ceased to be embarrassed with his squalid little room and his privation and became more free with her. She had become his friend.

She modelled for him for free. She was a good sitter. Sometimes, lost in the problem of getting some feature right he forgot to allow her periods of rest, and she just kept on sitting quietly, not daring to show her weariness and break his concentration. He worked carefully, lovingly, with intense care, to perfect that painting. He was never quite satisfied with the colour of her skin. And he took a long time to get the eyes quite right.

Finally he was satisfied. It was a masterpiece. He felt better than he had done for a long time, and she was pleased to see that he was happy with the result. He clasped her and kissed her on the cheek and laughed; and he used the little money he had to take her to a nightclub to celebrate the occasion.

After that he painted more frequently. The paintings were not good, but he kept working, and she visited him now and again, sometimes bringing books for him. He looked forward to her visits. And he worked hard to improve his painting; slowly it became better and once more he could get some satisfaction out of it.

Then one day she came to his studio and told him that she was going to be married. He stopped his painting and looked at her, shocked. He couldn't understand at first. To whom? When? She showed him the ring on her finger. Only two days ago she had got engaged, to a fellow she had been going with for nearly a year. He was a friend of the family, she added, and her parents approved of him. He was a businessman from the United States.

For the first time then he had tried to define his feelings for her. And he realized that he could never hope to get her. He knew what her parents were like; she didn't have to tell him. He knew her background. In the past, he had never mentioned love. Now he wanted to scream out that he was in love with her, didn't she realize it all the time - but he said nothing, could say nothing now. It was too late to raise this. He swallowed a bitter hurt and wished her all the best.

Neither did she mention any idea of love between the two of them. But she spoke as if in apology, as if trying to keep the hint of misery out of her voice. She was sure that she wouldn't regret the step she was taking; her fiancé was good to her. She talked a long time and he sensed that she knew that he was hurt. They sat silent for some time and then he again congratulated her and wished her all the best; and she left his room.

He saw her three times after that. Once she returned to his room to tell him that she would soon be going away, and that she would be married in New York. Once he saw her in a department store. And the last time he saw her, it was at an art exhibition and she walked in holding hands with a man. He watched them with interest; he was the sort of man who fitted exactly into Alison's class. They were a good match, he admitted to himself. He had tried to catch her eye but the gallery was crowded and she did not see him. All he could do was to point behind them and ask an acquaintance who the fellow was; the acquaintance said that he was Michael Norman.

The letter of a few days ago confirmed everything. Alison had written - as Mrs. Michael

Norman. She had also mentioned that they might be returning to the island soon. They were getting on well together. "We are very happy. Our second child is due soon..."

The artist stopped thinking, stopped staring at the wall. He imagined how surprised Alison would be when she saw the painting. He smiled, and got up from the armchair. He crossed the floor to the table and picked up the money scattered there. He pushed all the notes inside the table drawer; then he took out a dollar from the heap and went out to buy himself some cigarettes.

Essay on Communication: Dialect and Standard English

All communication and understanding come through language, spoken or written, and they are especially important in and among nations which claim to be democratic.

Now, this question of communication through language leads us into an area where, I know, we are full of doubt. We lack self-confidence about our naturally born, indigenous way of speech; often we condemn it, and wish that our language were different. I'm talking specifically about the current, constant and often unnecessary arguments about 'dialect' and 'Standard English'.

The truth is, our two ways of communication work quite well together, in their correct places, and if we seek to ban one or the other, we are seriously limiting ourselves. We cannot seek to remove either without changing our fundamental character, for, as Derek Walcott observed many years ago:

"To change our language we must change our life."

The proper assessment of ourselves that is so necessary to a vibrant nationhood cannot be made, unless we come to a fair and objective conclusion about our ways of expression and communication of ideas; and I believe that our failure, so far, to do this, is at the root of any lack of confidence we feel as a nation. If we keep condemning something about ourselves which cannot be removed, we will always be flying at half-mast. We will stumble and falter because we are trying to 'talk right'.

We would become tongue-tied, and give ourselves an impediment of speech that will kill discussion and ruin any national harmony that we might otherwise develop.

I am begging you, then, to come to an objective view about our 'dialect', one of our basic characteristics and resources; and I am suggesting that you are not Independent and Free unless you can communicate independently and freely, that is, without 'hang-ups'.

Now since you cannot analyse without facts, and since I know that generally we lack facts about language to guide us in our analysis of it, and since instinctively I am a teacher, I will have to lay out some brief and basic ideas about language in general, and about our language in particular.

Communication is for transmitting ideas. There is a very definite pattern to communication. An idea comes to your mind, which you want to share. Speaking and writing are the two means of transmitting ideas, and writing is more formal, less original, than speaking. Speaking came, and comes, first.

Your listener(s) must understand the language you speak if the idea is to be received from your mouth into their brains. Or, you have to talk in a language that they understand best, and most quickly. Speaking carries with it tone, emotional content, gestures, and so on, which help to carry the meaning. In our society, 'dialect' conveys more immediate meaning than 'standard English'; but generally, speaking does this more than writing can./Some people who can write well cannot speak well; some people who can speak well cannot write well. We need to be able to do both well, and in both dialect and Standard English'; but it is far more important, in our present circumstances, to be able to write English well, however we speak; and I hope you take careful note of that.

The more ways a person can find to communicate, the better it is for that person's self-expression; if you can speak Bajan to Bajans, French to the French, German to the Germans and Swahili to the Swahili speaker, you are very lucky. Language can be condemned only if it is used in inappropriate circumstances. You should understand this very clearly.

Talking in Dialect

Talking in dialect obviously is not 'speaking badly' when Bajans are communicating among themselves. Indeed, our method of oral communication (I will talk about written dialect later) is most convenient and suited to the task of informing Bajans about themselves. It is for communicating to our own about our own; and it relates back to the Discussion that occurs among the people of a nation, about their past, present and future actions, if they say that they are democratic, independent and free.

Being polite and humane on the personal level obeying the norms and laws of the society even if there is disagreement with some of them, and being truthful but wise in both internal and external affairs, is as necessary to an individual as it is to a nation, and should be a natural, right-feeling and confident part of our nature, if we say that we are individually and nationally independent and free.

To get the maximum good out of such behaviour, even to achieve it, involves quick transmittal and understanding of ideas./What you say is more important than how you say it; in fact, you should not talk, as many people do, unless you have something to say. (This applies to writing, too).

The language you use in an emergency, when communication has to be made with no frills attached, is your true language. You see then that English is 'put on'; dialect is natural, spontaneous.

Dialect is a serious mode of national communication, and it must not be bandied about. That foolish, brawling kind of orality which many local actors assume to 'dialect' makes a mockery of our language – and no language should be mocked. The assumption that it smacks of low-life, immorality and ignorance, and that it is laced with cuss-words, is disgraceful, and more so when we know for sure that at all levels of society, Bajans at home or in informal situations talk Bajan most of the time.

Prejudice against Language

Some of us act as though we are cursed by being saddled with such a way of talking. Despising the dialect is a strange and virulent kind of self-hatred and a hatred of the facts of nature themselves; for it is nature that has made us as we are.

What nature has done, obviously, should be accepted by human beings; for we are products of that very nature.

Prejudice against language is not natural; it is taught. (Thus self-hatred, nature-hatred, is taught). A young child communicates without pondering about the way he/she communicates without pondering about the way he/she communicates. If both speaker and listener are concerned about the subject, the way in which it is rendered is scarcely noticed.

When we have an idea and we resort to attempting to transmit it in 'good English', without knowing enough about 'good English' to succeed (and believe, nowadays few school or university students know 'good English'), we are damaging ourselves psychologically; creating an unnecessary blockage. We are not using language according to its true purpose, which is to communicate.

Three Nation-Builders

A false, negative and unfair attitude towards our indigenous language does not build an independent and free nation; for the three chief things that build a nation are, a homeland, an historic tradition, and a common language.

Again, some of us prefer another homeland, historic tradition and language ... another race, even. Such people suffer a terrible frustration, and I am sorry for them.

Emancipation is not simply a political matter; it is a mental state. If we accept others more than we accept ourselves, we are (still) mentally enslaved. And as brother Nesta Bob Marley says:

"Emancipate yourselves from mental slavery:
None but ourselves can free our minds."

Talking freely

Your mind is not free unless you can talk freely, without labouring over the technique of talking. You know (or can imagine) how mentally frustrating it is, would be, if you knew very little Spanish and you had to explain something very important to, say, a companero from Cuba who knew only his form of Spanish (this actually happened to me). Consider how puzzled an Englishman looks, or would look, if you talked to him, in England, in the dialect of Barbados.

You should talk in the language that is most certain to be understood by your listener.

Towards two common languages

'Bajan' is common to all Barbadians; as children, they learnt it, you must be aware. You must be aware, too, of the fact that Standard English is not common to all Barbadians. Don't get me wrong; I truly regret this fact. We should be masters in the use of English; we should be proud of being able, when we want, to use the Englishman's language equally as well, or better, than he.

We assume that we know Standard English because our dialect employs English words; we fail to understand that language is built on Structure rather than words, and because we think we know English, we fail to examine the structural side of Standard English, - I mean the grammar, tenses, position of words, etc. – and to compare it with the structure of our local language.

Considering how hard the teachers of English Language in this island have worked, I say it is a shame that we are not masters of the English language ... and, simultaneously, confident users of our own speech.

Knowing only one and not the other is placing a serious limitation on yourself.

I treat all language (and all forms of communication) equally, for I see them for what they are: tools for transmitting important ideas to others.

A tool does not exist for its own sake; it is there to be used; and the more skilful you are in the use of tools, the better your project will work out.

Tools are used on materials; and we all know that materials should not be wasted.

With speaking and writing, this means that words must be used economically, with the maximum impact that you can create; it means too that you must seek to render your ideas as quickly and clearly as possible.

This principle applies to writing more forcibly than it applies to speaking, however. When you are speaking and your listener fails to understand, he can ask questions (unless, of course, you've been recorded or are speaking on radio, TV, or such like). When you are writing, your reader has no such opportunity.

Listening, Reading, Writing and Understanding

Listening is easier than reading. Writing is a more technical mode of communicating than speaking is. We have to be sure that we are not puzzling our readers by placing obstacles to understanding in their path. We must not glory in the use of 'big words'; if we do, it serves us right if the reader throws away our piece of writing in disgust. If a reader fails to understand, it is usually the fault of the writer, who most likely is trying to mesmerize the reader with his so-called intellect.

Writing the Spoken

The latest technical problem our writers have is how to put our oral language into written form. I will explain how this can best be done, but first, I must answer the question, why attempt to write dialect at all?

Well, if we are recording the way of life of our people, especially in fiction, we need to use 'characters'. These characters have to talk in order to bring immediacy and life to our writing; often a character is understood through what he says and how he says it.

The Process of Reading – Ease and Difficulty

Reading involves seeing and recognising words, as we will notice when we watch small children learning to read. When handwriting is very bad, when the writing is in a language we do not know, when words are mis-spelt or the writing is unfamiliar for any reason, the process of seeing and recognising is severely curtailed.

Under such conditions, a reader is hampered by slow and painful attempts at comprehension. He has to translate before he can comprehend, and he persists in his attempts to comprehend only because of his pathetic and often futile faith in the writer.

Often I have heard people say, "I cannot read dialect". I have discovered that the main reason for this is that dialect-writers spoil their work by the purposeful mis-spelling of the words. They take delight in personal, whimsical spellings of words. They accept the view that dialect is strictly an uneducated way of talking, and they try to reflect the un-education of the dialect-speaker by the corruption of normal, standard spelling.

Let me point out that standard spelling is not the same as Standard English. The mis-spelling of words does not enhance, but detracts from, the art of dialect-writing, and writers who purposefully mis-spell are doing a disservice to the dialect, and to their own chances of being accepted by the general populace, who even if talking dialect, know how to spell, if they can read.

So if I write: **'I gwine dong de rode'**, even a dialect-speaker might misunderstand; but if I write: **'I going down the road'**, there is no misunderstanding.

A little study will show you, then, that writing 'good' dialect is to do with the structure or rhythm of the language rather than with the spelling of words. No reader is interested in attempts at phonetic spelling. When the words are spelt in normal fashion, and a

Barbadian reads them aloud, his intonation supplies the sound required to establish the dialect. (Frank Collymore, peace be unto him, pointed all this out many years ago.)

Intonation is important; in fact, Barbadian intonations make people think that a Barbadian speaking Standard English is speaking dialect. Sometimes we condemn our very intonation ... a sad state.

Our problem is not unique; wherever there has been colonialism there is a standard official language and a local dialect, and one is regarded as more international than the other, and rightly so. Still, I know few nations where there is such a strong aversion to the local language among some natives as occurs in Barbados.

Dialect is not 'broken English', but a clever compromise between several different African languages and English; we really should be quite proud of having managed so well linguistically, over the centuries.

No limitations to Dialect

Again, many dialect speakers assume that 'big words' cannot occur in dialect. Thus, they limit themselves. Good writing calls for using the appropriate words, and all the words you know can be utilised in your writing. So if I write

"I going expatiate 'pon certain linguistic principles",

that is dialect–writing, too.

This removes the argument that dialect is limited in its use, and cannot record the whole range of our experience. Any language can record the experience of its speakers, and if they have a new experience, they create new words.

In writing any language, you search for the right words to convey your meaning, and any word in your vocabulary is at your disposal.

Teachers and Dialect

Some teachers have been accused of teaching dialect in schools. It's a ridiculous accusation. Dialect does not have to be taught; Standard English has to be.

Unthinking teachers often reinforce prejudice against the dialect by demanding that pupils not speak it. This places a serious limitation on a child who has not yet learnt to express ideas and needs in Standard English; it can ruin his self-confidence for life.

Again, some teachers fear that a story written in dialect, however, correct the spelling, will somehow lessen the child's chances of learning Standard English. They fail to see that they can use the dialect to improve the child's grasp of Standard English, simply by resorting to objective comparison of the two modes of communication. Often, too, teachers pay too much attention to the mode of communication, and too little to the themes and plots of stories – where the most important elements lie.

If a story is well written and told, a listener or reader, at the end of it, will scarcely remember whether it was written/told in dialect or Standard English.

Teachers, you must try this exercise, get a piece of dialect-writing, and ask your pupils to translate it into Standard English. The task will be extremely beneficial, to both you and them.

Being able to communicate with confidence with the tools of your communication makes you free to concentrate on what you want to say (or write); but this condition cannot come about unless you are fluent and fearless in your methods of communication. Speaking independently and freely, then, is easy and a laudable goal.

Profile of

Author Timothy Callender

...as told by others

"He was in the forefront of our literary advance and his (dialect) literature restored respectability to Barbadian life."- **John Wickham – Nation newspaper Literary Editor**

"Easily the best exponent of the art of short story writing Barbados has ever had...he uses the vernacular as one should apply seasoning to flying fish...discretely to bring out taste, and not inordinately to spoil the enjoyment of the diner..."- **E.L Cozier, *Topic for Today* – Barbados Advocate.. Oct., '87**

"I hope that Barbadians always remember him for the joy he brought to them through his writing."- **Alfred Pragnell – Storyteller**

"He won NIFCA awards for short stories, poetry and drama" - **National Independence Festival of Creative Arts (NIFCA) pays tribute to late author – October 1989.**

"Callender's goal was to create literature that can stand up to any critical analysis and yet can be familiarly and naturally read and understood by the people of his own environment, including children.." -**Dean Harold Crichlow, *Preface to Callender's booklet* 'Independence & Freedom'**

"I think that his writing encouraged a person to view Bajan dialect in a more positive way and to see local life as something which was a worthy subject for literature."- **John Gilmore, Association of Literary Writers – 1989**

"He was a sculptor, artist, painter, playwright, novelist, poet, photographer, teacher and an accomplished guitarist (and drummer)- **Barbados Advocate, Oct. 1989**

"He had an overall enchantment with the melodic speech rhythms of Caribbean people." **Dawn Morgan, Columnist, Nation newspaper**

"His work stands head and shoulders above most of his peers and contemporaries"….**Mighty Gabby, Calypsonian and Social Commentator.**

"Timothy Callender had an amazing intellect. His short stories were culled from the people around him and thru them helped to define for me what was Bajan." **Elton 'Elombe' Mottley – Director, Yoruba House and Director of NIFCA, Cultural Advocate.**

"The man stands for so many things and is so much to so many people." **Andy Taitt, Co-owner, *The Bookplace & Literary Reviewer***

"He was more than an educator. He was a sculptor, artist, painter, playwright, novelist, poet, photographer, teacher and an accomplished guitarist and pianist." **Barbados Advocate newspaper Oct'89**

Also available at Amazon.com

IT SO HAPPEN 16 Short Stories in Kindle and Print edition

IT SO HAPPEN 2 – Christmas Stories – Kindle edition

SEARCHERS, SECRETS and SILENCES – a detective thriller in verse - Kindle edition

HOW MUSIC CAME TO THE AINCHAN PEOPLE – classic epic novel - Print and Kindle editions

Soon available
**IT SO HAPPEN 4 – Tales of the Caribbean – Historical & Hysterical
ELEMENTS OF ART – a manual for the Creative Arts
IT SO HAPPEN 5 – Callender's Funniest Short Stories**

Proof

Made in the USA
Charleston, SC
28 May 2013